Calculator Activities

Written by Martin Blows and Jane Porter

Published by Scholastic Publications Ltd,
Villiers House, Clarendon Avenue,
Leamington Spa, Warwickshire CV32 5PR

© 1992 Scholastic Publications Ltd

Written by Martin Blows and Jane Porter
Edited by Janet Fisher
Sub-edited by Kim Daniel and
Catherine Baker
Illustrations by Jane Bottomley and
Chris Saunderson
Front and back covers designed by
Sue Limb
Photograph by Martyn Chillmaid
Artwork by Liz Preece, Castle Graphics,
Kenilworth

Printed in Great Britain by Loxley Brothers
Ltd, Sheffield

**British Library Cataloguing in
Publication Data**
A catalogue record for this book is
available from the British Library.

ISBN 0 590 53015 1

Contents

Introduction

The use of the calculator in the primary school is not a recent phenomenon introduced as a result of the National Curriculum for mathematics. Work has been developing since the early 1970s when calculators became cheap enough for primary schools to purchase in quantity. However, it was the Cockcroft Report in 1982 that placed the calculator firmly on the primary agenda:

'In our view, more [work] is needed both to consider the use of calculators as an aid to teaching and learning within the primary mathematics curriculum as a whole and also the extent to which arithmetical aspects of the curriculum may need to be modified.'

(*Mathematics Counts*,
(The Cockcroft Report) para. 338,
HMSO 1982)

CALCULATORS AND THE PRIMARY CURRICULUM

These suggestions were again supported in the 1985 HMI document *Curriculum Matters 3: Mathematics from 5 to 16* which laid the foundations for the later National Curriculum documents:

'A policy of allowing pupils to use a calculator is not sufficient. What is needed is a school policy which encourages pupils of all ages and abilities to use calculators in appropriate situations and provides clear guidance on the procedures needed to obtain maximum benefit from their use.'
(*Mathematics from 5 to 16*, HMSO 1985)

The National Curriculum for mathematics has now made the use of the calculator an important part of every child's education; not just for checking answers, but for developing children's mathematical ability and understanding. In some instances, children *must* be able to use a calculator, whilst in others the choice is left to them. There are relatively few mathematical activities which definitely preclude their use.

CALCULATORS AND NUMBER SKILLS

This does, of course, raise queries from teachers, parents and governors who regard the calculator as a threat to children's numeracy skills. However, calculators are unlikely to be a threat if they are used sensibly, not just for checking longhand answers, but as another teaching aid for motivating and encouraging success in mathematics.

There is also growing evidence to suggest that calculators are a powerful tool in the improvement of children's computational ability:

'From all the studies the weight of evidence is strong that the use of calculators has not produced any adverse effect on basic computational ability.'
(*Mathematics Counts*
(The Cockcroft Report)
para. 377, HMSO 1982)

The recent PRIME project (Primary Initiatives in Mathematical Education) explored in depth the results of allowing children free use of calculators from an early age. The CAN (Calculators Aware Number) Curriculum, part of the PRIME project, discovered that, far from reducing children's understanding in mathematics, free access to calculators has enhanced children's ability to handle numbers and their understanding of the number system itself.

Although parents will often suggest that 'calculators rot the brain', they will generally acknowledge that they use one themselves, either at home or at work. A more structured approach to their use is needed within the classroom, so that children can gain maximum benefit from them.

The calculator does not, however, make the learning of number bonds redundant. It is still quicker to know from recall that seven eights are fifty-six than to find a calculator and key in the problem. The National Curriculum assessment guidance makes this very clear. However, a full integration of the calculator into maths lessons means less time spent on computational exercises, and more time for activities to aid the understanding of place value, number pattern and the meaningful use of mathematics in problem-solving situations.

It is important to acknowledge that the calculator can perform some mathematical operations far more quickly than we can. Calculators are a part of our technological age, and we cannot ignore their existence

and their effect on what we teach. Some of the old algorithms – like those for long division, devised for clerks working in the pre-calculator era – are no longer relevant in today's electronic age.

That does not mean children should not understand the process of equal sharing or repeated subtraction which lies behind calculations based on division. But they should be encouraged to use their own methods of recording which they fully understand and can remember for occasions when they are without a calculator.

'. . . only very basic and simple calculations need now be done on paper; some standard written methods of calculation, such as long division, which many pupils find difficult and few really understand, should no longer be generally taught. To use a calculator only to check written calculations is inappropriate but to use mental or simple written approximations to check results obtained from a calculator is sensible.'
(*Mathematics from 5 to 16*, HMSO 1985)

THE IMPORTANCE OF MENTAL METHODS
The ability to use simple mental methods or approximations actually demands a considerable understanding of number, pattern and relationships. There is an obvious need to balance the apparently conflicting, but mutually supportive, elements of mental and calculator-powered arithmetic. The notion that calculators will turn children into 'unthinking button-pushers' is far from the truth. A calculator does not tell you what sums to do, which buttons to press, or whether the final answer is likely to be right. These are still the child's decisions, and as such still need to be covered in teaching.

'We wish to stress that the availability of a calculator in no way reduces the need for mathematical understanding on the part of the person who is using it.'
(*Mathematics Counts* (The Cockcroft Report) para. 378, HMSO 1982)

THE CALCULATOR-CONSCIOUS CURRICULUM
The National Curriculum for mathematics has introduced new areas into the primary curriculum and has changed the emphasis of others, particularly the reinforcement of often misunderstood algorithms such as those for fractions, percentages and long division. The use of the calculator in these areas will give teachers more time to work with pupils on a better understanding of place value, mental facility and number awareness, as well as a chance to investigate new areas such as directed numbers and trial and improvement methods, highlighted by the use of the calculator. Finally, the calculator will allow children to begin to explore the real world in which they live. Real prices, measurements and situations become starting points for problem-solving investigations which will help to give children a feeling for, and an understanding of, mathematics.

CALCULATOR SKILLS
Behind this greater use of the calculator must be an understanding of how it works and how to use it. This needs to be taught, not necessarily in a systematic lesson format on a Tuesday morning, but through activities and games which provide a context for the use of, say, the constant function or the percentage key.

Correct use of the calculator should be encouraged at all times. Children do not need to use longhand calculations first, or double-check every calculation, but they should check the display to see that digits have been entered correctly, they should know how to make simple corrections and, most importantly of all, they should check that their answers are realistic and reasonable in the context of the problem. Calculators, like computers, are no more reliable than their operator! Children should question every answer and not accept it just because it is in the calculator display.

INTEGRATING THE CALCULATOR INTO THE CURRICULUM

The calculator should not be considered as a special treat for the end of term or for filling odd moments, nor should it appear as a set lesson. It should become part of the teacher's tools, like Cuisinaire rods, abacuses and multi-base equipment, which is used when appropriate and when needed by the child.

There is no need for every child to have a calculator. A few in every class with a central resource to make a half- or full-class set will cater for most needs. However, a school policy for purchasing calculators for use throughout the school is essential. Many activities which include using a calculator are more beneficial if children work in pairs. By discussing what they are doing, the children will understand more easily.

CALCULATORS AND THE NATIONAL CURRICULUM

The emphasis given to the use of a calculator within the programmes of study for mathematics clearly highlights its importance within the National Curriculum. The non-statutory guidance also provides a useful rationale for integrating calculators into the curriculum:

'In learning to use calculators, pupils should have the opportunity to:
● become familiar with the number operations to be performed by calculators as they progress through the levels of Attainment Targets 2 and 3 [now Attainment Target 2];
● explore the way a calculator works through a variety of number games and similar activities;
● develop confidence in selecting correct key sequences for various calculations;
● use mental methods to estimate for expected answers, check for reasonableness and interpret results;
● use calculators as a powerful means of exploring numbers and to extend their understanding of the nature of numbers and number relationships.'
(*Mathematics in the National Curriculum* – Non-Statutory Guidance)

USING THIS BOOK

This book does not provide a course in calculator use, but it does aim to present a development of ideas and a range of uses for the calculator. It also highlights the increased importance of calculators in the National Curriculum.

At the simplest level the calculator can be used to check answers, but a more appropriate use is to aid the development of a range of number skills using a 'forecast and check' mode. This can often be used initially to provide a set of answers which will help children to spot a pattern and make further calculations easier.

Games are a great motivator, and the activities contain many examples which can be used to help children develop a concept or skill. Some of the best calculator games can be used many times over, with different levels of difficulty or new challenges added as children's number understanding grows.

Many of the activities require children to make written records as they go along. This provides teachers with some evidence about what has happened and where mistakes were made. Some of the activities are almost impossible without recording; for example, with trial and improvement ideas you soon lose track of the numbers tried if you don't keep a written record.

A written record can often be useful in diagnosing areas of misunderstanding. In one-to-one situations the calculator will often give a child enough confidence to demonstrate what he has done, or explain how he arrived at a certain answer. Like the computer, the calculator is an unthreatening aid to thought and can actually foster and encourage discussion about mathematics.

Most of the activities provide starting points for further development. Some need little prior preparation of materials, but others will need photocopied sheets, or examples to get children started. Most can be developed by using larger or smaller numbers and can be revisited when appropriate as pupils' understanding grows. Other activities will provide you with initial ideas from which a range of similar activities or games can be developed. Children will often invent their own extensions.

Although some of the activities in the first chapter may be appropriate for older pupils, they are also intended for teachers. If you are still unsure or hesitant about which keys to press or which buttons do what, use the ideas yourself and try them out. You may get a few surprises!

We hope that the book will give you a greater understanding of the way in which the calculator can enhance your children's mathematics, and at the same time provide a source of practical ideas to use in the classroom.

1. Getting to know your calculator

Calculators come in many shapes and sizes and, while they may appear to perform the same basic tasks, there are often differences beneath the keypad.

This chapter is designed to help both teachers and older children discover more about how their calculators work. You will need to decide which activities are appropriate for your children.

The most common type of calculator used in primary schools is the simple four-function calculator. It is useful if all the children in the class have the same make of calculator, if not the same model number, as the conventions tend to alter between manufacturers rather than between particular models. However, you are likely to end up with some different makes, simply because children will bring their own to school. This chapter will help you to explain to children the differences between calculators, particularly if they bring in their older brothers' and sisters' scientific calculators. We hope it will also give you confidence to explore your own calculator and to make better use of it, both in your teaching and in your own mathematics.

1. What does what?

Age range
Nine to eleven, and teachers.

Group size
Pairs or small groups.

What you need
Calculators, pencils, photocopiable page 101.

What to do
Give each pair or group a photocopy of the calculator check sheet. This sheet shows a calculator with a combination of keys not normally found on any one simple calculator, but it helps to illustrate many important points.

Ask the children to match up the words in the box with the lines indicating the parts of the calculator. Use their results to discuss the names of the keys and parts of the calculator.

Some particular conventions are worth noting:
● The separate numerals which appear in the display screen are always called digits.
● The add, subtract, divide and multiply keys are called function or operator keys. They are also known as binary operators because they need two numbers to work.
● Keys like the square root or percentage are known as unary operators. They need only one number.
● There may be three or four memory keys.
● The clear buttons will vary from make to make. There may be one button marked ON/C or C/CE or two marked C and AC. There are other variations, too.

2. Talking about calculator keys

Age range
Seven to eleven, and teachers.

Group size
Pairs or small groups.

What you need
One calculator between two, photocopiable page 102 (the calculator vocabulary sheet).

What to do
Give each pair a photocopy of the calculator vocabulary sheet. Tell them to match the words given to the appropriate boxes around the calculator. Encourage the children to discuss their work with each other.

Use the results as a basis for talking about mathematical vocabulary. Some points are worth noting:

• The zero key should not be called 'oh'. It is a numeric key and not a letter of the alphabet. Try to get children (and teachers) into the habit of using either zero or nought.

• The decimal point key looks like a dot, but children should refer to it as a decimal point.

• The equals key may also be called a totals key, particularly when children make repeated additions.

• There is a wide range of terms used for each of the four function keys. Encourage the children to use the appropriate language, for example, the 'divide' key rather than the 'share by' key!

Follow-up
When the sheets have been completed, ask the children to fill in the missing number keys without looking at a calculator. Notice that all numeric keypads start with the number 1 at the bottom left-hand corner. Compare that with a telephone keypad! Does anyone know why they are different?

3. A case of logic

Age range
Ten to eleven, and teachers.

Group size
Small groups.

What you need
One calculator between two.

Background
The simple calculators found in most homes are four-function calculators. They can be identified as such by their relatively low number of keys and cost. Scientific calculators may have 20 or more different keys with labels such as $\boxed{\tan}$, $\boxed{\log}$, etc. They are used in secondary schools onwards and although they *can* be used in primary classrooms, they are not the most suitable for younger pupils.

Although calculators basically look the same, they do not all operate in the same way. There are two different types of calculator logic in common use. Simple calculators use arithmetic logic; scientific calculators use algebraic logic. The following activity is intended to show the difference between the two.

What to do
Ask the children to key in the following:
4 $\boxplus$ 2 $\boxtimes$ 5 $\boxminus$

An algebraic logic (scientific) calculator will give the answer 14. It rewrites the expression as a mathematician would by taking the multiplication part first:
$$4 + (2 \times 5) = 14$$

With arithmetic logic, in a simple calculator, the expression is worked out in the order it is entered:
$$4 + 2 \times 5 = 30$$

Both are right! They simply use different logic systems to sort out the answer. If children bring in their own calculators, some of which may be scientific ones, problems could arise. However, you could use the differences to introduce the idea of order of priorities for calculations.

Follow-up
Discuss with the children why problems may arise with a scientific calculator and how they can get around them. The solution is to press the equals key $\boxminus$ between each calculation. The example given would be keyed as:
4 $\boxplus$ 2 $\boxminus$ $\boxtimes$ 5 $\boxminus$ 30

The calculator has to work out the sum at each step rather than waiting until the end and applying priority to the order of operations.

Also, ask the children to work out how the simple calculator can give the same answer as the scientific one. The multiplication and division have to be done before the addition and subtraction. Children may need to understand how brackets are used before they can do this.
4 $\boxplus$ (2 $\boxtimes$ 5) $\boxminus$ 14

Alternatively, you can re-write the sum to give the algebraic answer:
2 $\boxtimes$ 5 $\boxplus$ 4 $\boxminus$ 14

4. The constant function

Age range
Six to eleven, and teachers.

Group size
Pairs or small groups.

What you need
One calculator between two.

Background
The constant function is a useful facility which allows the same operation to be repeated many times on a starting number by pressing only a single key each time. It is useful for building up tables, working with number lines, counting backwards and forwards in stages, finding squares, dividing by repeated subtraction and multiplying by repeated addition.

Unfortunately, calculator manufacturers cannot agree on the operation of this facility, and there are two major formats on the market.

What to do
The task is to make the calculator add on 2 from the starting number 6 by using a constant of add 2. Try making the add constant in the following ways:

Method 1
Key in:
6 ⊞ 2 ⊟ ⊟ ⊟ giving 8, 10, 12
The constant is created by repeatedly pressing the ⊟ key. If all you get is 8 (the sum is done just once) don't worry, try the second method.

Method 2
This method works the other way around; the constant is entered first and the starting number added after:
2 ⊞ ⊞ 6 ⊟ ⊟ ⊟ giving 8, 10, 12
Here, the constant is created by pressing the ⊞ key twice in succession. A 'constant in use' sign (k) will usually appear in the display with this type of calculator.

The first method is simpler to follow and is more easily understood by children. However, it is possible to set up a constant without meaning to, by simply pressing the ⊟ key too many times.

Method 3 (Universal method)
Problems will arise where there are some of each type of calculator in a group or class. These can be alleviated by using a slightly longer approach which works on all calculators. The constant is set by keying:
2 ⊞ ⊞ ⊟ 0
This makes a constant of 2 and a starting number of 0. By keying in the number you want to start from next, you can add in twos from that number.
2 ⊞ ⊞ ⊟ 0 10 ⊟ ⊟ ⊟ gives 12, 14, 16
The constant will stay set until you press AC. If you want to count on from a different number, simply type in the new starting number from wherever you are and press the ⊟ key. There is no need to clear the last number from the display.

When the children have mastered the constant function, ask them to try the following list of examples on two different makes of calculator. They should use the constant function to produce the following sequences, making a note of the keys they press:
- 1, 2, 3, 4, 5 . . .
- 2, 4, 6, 8 . . .
- 0, 2, 4, 6, 8 . . .
- 1, 3, 5, 7 . . .

Younger children might need help at first but they will quickly learn how to set up a constant. A 'constant reminder' chart on the classroom wall will help them if they forget. There is an example of such a chart opposite.

When using constants, try to ensure that all the calculators are the same make so that the constant is always set up in the same way.

Follow-up

The multiplication constant method is the same for all calculators, with the constant entered first. For division, the place of the constant again depends on the make of calculator. You will need to experiment with your own

A Constant Reminder

Method 1
Start number $\boxed{+}$ constant $\boxed{=}$ $\boxed{=}$ $\boxed{=}$

Method 2
Constant $\boxed{+}$ $\boxed{+}$ Start number $\boxed{=}$ $\boxed{=}$ $\boxed{=}$

Universal Method
Constant $\boxed{+}$ $\boxed{+}$ $\boxed{=}$ $\bigcirc$ Start number $\boxed{=}$ $\boxed{=}$ $\boxed{=}$

calculator to see whether the constant is the first or second number entered. Older children might like to check this out:

Multiplication

2 $\boxed{\times}$ $\boxed{\times}$ 10 $\boxed{=}$ $\boxed{=}$ $\boxed{=}$ gives 20, 40, 80 . . .
10 $\boxed{\times}$ $\boxed{\times}$ 2 $\boxed{=}$ $\boxed{=}$ $\boxed{=}$ gives 20, 200, 2000 . . .

Division
Either:

2 $\boxed{\div}$ $\boxed{\div}$ 10 $\boxed{=}$ $\boxed{=}$ $\boxed{=}$ gives 0.2, 0.02, 0.002 . . .
10 $\boxed{\div}$ $\boxed{\div}$ 2 $\boxed{=}$ $\boxed{=}$ $\boxed{=}$ gives 5, 2.5, 1.25 . . .

or:

2 $\boxed{\div}$ $\boxed{\div}$ 10 $\boxed{=}$ $\boxed{=}$ $\boxed{=}$ gives 5, 2.5, 1.25 . . .
10 $\boxed{\div}$ $\boxed{\div}$ 2 $\boxed{=}$ $\boxed{=}$ $\boxed{=}$ gives 0.2, 0.02, 0.002 . . .

Can the children explain what is happening in each case?

Let them try the following list for practice, making a note of the keys they press to produce each sequence.

- 2, 4, 8, 16 . . .
- 100, 107, 114, 121 . . .
- 1 000 000, 100 000, 10 000 . . .
- 5, −5, 5, −5 . . .
- −3, −6, −9, −12 . . .

5. Negative numbers

Age range
Seven to eleven, and teachers.

Group size
Individuals or pairs.

What you need
One calculator between two.

Background
The simple four-function calculators in current use vary quite markedly as to where the negative sign indicator is placed.

What to do
Ask the children to key in a simple sum that will give a negative number as the answer:

4 ⊟ 7 ⊟

An answer of negative 3 should be displayed. Check where the negative sign is positioned. It may be found:

- just in front of the number;

	− 3

- on the extreme left of the number;

−	3

- or in many cases behind the number.

	3 −

The first example is the clearest and most natural mathematical position.

-1 -2 -3 -4 -5 -6

Follow-up
On some calculators an operator sign appears in the display behind the number after an operator button is pressed. These symbols can be useful, as they remind children what operation will be performed when the equals key is pressed. However, it is important that children do not confuse the minus sign indicator with a negative number indicator. On such calculators the negative number indicator usually appears just in front of the number.

6. Correcting mistakes

Age range
Six to eleven, and teachers.

Group size
Pairs or small groups.

What you need
One calculator between two.

Background
Many calculator users are unaware that they can make corrections to calculations as they go along. You might want to change the operation from addition to subtraction because you have used the wrong key or else you might want to alter the last number entered if you have keyed it incorrectly or chosen the wrong one from a list. Both are possible without having to start again.

What to do

Tell the children that they are going to do the sum 23 + 45.

Operator corrections

Ask them to key in the following:

$2\ 3\ \boxminus$

they need to change the $\boxminus$ to $\boxplus$. This is easy. They must simply press the correct operator key and continue with the problem. The key presses would be:

$2\ 3\ \boxminus\ \boxplus\ 4\ 5\ \boxminus$

The operator mistake can be corrected at any time until the next number is entered. After that, the correction is more difficult.

Number corrections

It is also possible to correct a mistake with a number that you are entering. However, calculators differ in dealing with this.

● Some have two separate keys, which may be $\boxed{C}$ and $\boxed{AC}$. In this case, the $\boxed{AC}$ key clears the whole calculator, including the memory. The $\boxed{C}$ key lets you clear the last number entered.

● Other calculators have a single button marked $\boxed{C/CE}$. Here you press the key once to clear an entry and twice to clear the entire calculation. In some cases the clear button is shared with the on button $\boxed{ON/C}$; one press clears the last entry and two presses will clear the entire calculator.

If your calculator has a different combination of keys, experiment to see what happens.

Forearmed with this information, ask the children to try the same but make a mistake when they reach the second number:

$2\ 3\ \boxplus\ 4\ 7$

Make sure they stop after the 47 and don't press $\boxminus$. To alter the 47 to 45, either one of these methods will work, depending on the calculator:

$2\ 3\ \boxplus\ 4\ 7\ \boxed{C}\ 4\ 5\ \boxminus$

or

$2\ 3\ \boxplus\ 4\ 7\ \boxed{C/CE}\ 4\ 5\ \boxminus$

The important thing to remember is that the last number can only be changed before the next operator key is pressed. If you press either an operator or equals key the calculation will be complete.

Note that after pressing $\boxed{C}$ to clear a number entry, some displays will show the last number entered and others will show 0 on the display. Both are correct.

Follow-up

Give the children lots of practice with this facility so that they know how to make corrections with different calculators.

2.2360679

7. Square roots

Age range
Ten to eleven, and teachers.

Group size
Individuals or pairs.

What you need
One calculator between two.

What to do
Children often ask what the square root key does. Try turning the question into an investigation.

Ask children to try some numbers. Start with numbers that have perfect square roots.

4 $\boxed{\sqrt{}}$ (Note there is no need to press equals.)
How did the calculator arrive at the answer 2?

9 $\boxed{\sqrt{}}$
How did it get 3?

Carry on trying other numbers, and encourage the children to come up with their own definition of a square root.

Follow-up
It is also possible to find the square root of other numbers by trial and improvement methods. See Chapter 6, page 69 for more information on this.

8. Squares and powers

Age range
Ten to eleven, and teachers.

Group size
Individuals or pairs.

What you need
One calculator between two.

What to do
Some calculators will have a key marked $\boxed{x^2}$. To use this to square a number simply enter the number and press the $\boxed{x^2}$ key:

3 $\boxed{x^2}$ will give 9.

If the calculator doesn't have a $\boxed{x^2}$ key you can use the constant function to do the same thing:

3 $\boxed{\times}$ $\boxed{=}$ will give 9.

To raise a number to the power of 4 (2^4) you need to set a multiply by 2 constant:

2 $\boxed{\times}$ $\boxed{\times}$ $\boxed{=}$ $\boxed{=}$ $\boxed{=}$ will always give $2^4 = 16$

Follow-up
Children will be fascinated to see numbers grow in this way. The ease with which numbers can be raised to any power will enable them to explore number patterns in a new way.

9. Dealing with decimals

Age range
Ten to eleven, and teachers.

Group size
Pairs or small groups.

What you need
One calculator between two.

Background
Most simple calculators only have space for eight digits on the display screen. However, the calculator must be able to deal with numbers that have a decimal fraction. The simple calculator truncates numbers which it cannot fit on to the screen. A scientific calculator rounds and preserves the accuracy of the answer.

What to do
Ask the children to key in:
1 ÷ 6 =
They will probably get 0.1666666. The calculator has merely cut off the line of decimals, taking no account of the rules for rounding numbers. This is called truncation. If the children make the reverse calculation:
0.1666666 × 6 =
. . . they will probably arrive at an answer of 0.9999996. This is because the calculator has not rounded the number and has discarded any extra figures it could not fit into the display.

If this exercise is repeated using a scientific calculator, the calculator will round the last digit to display 0.1666667 (a rounded answer). If you do the reverse operation on a scientific calculator, you will get back to the starting number.

Follow-up
● The same problem will occur on a simple calculator if you try to find the square root of a number which isn't a perfect square, such as 15. If you then square the answer you will not get back to the original number.
● Most basic calculators have a floating decimal point which appears in different places according to the number being displayed. In this way both 0.123456 and 12345.6 can be shown. If the point was fixed to two decimal places the first number would be shown as 0.12.

10. Memory

Age range
Ten to eleven, and teachers.

Group size
Individuals or pairs.

What you need
One calculator between two.

Background
Most four-function calculators now have a memory. There should be at least three memory keys. These will be M+ (add to memory), M− (subtract from memory) and MR (memory recall). A fourth memory key, MC, will clear the memory contents only.

The memory can be useful for more complicated calculations, storing a number for repeated use, or storing answers to parts of a calculation.

What to do

To solve the problem $(28 \times 83) - (25 \times 62)$ without using the memory you would need to write down the answer to (28×83) before calculating (25×62). The first answer would then have to be re-entered for the final calculation.

The memory can be used to shorten this process. The first part is calculated and stored in the memory:
28 ⊠ 83 ⊟ M+

Although this part can be cleared from the display by pressing C (not AC as this would also clear the memory), this is not necessary since as soon as you start to enter the second part, the first part will be automatically cleared because the ⊟ key will have been pressed.

Now ask the children to enter the second part:
25 ⊠ 62 ⊟ and subtract from the total in memory M−

The final answer, 774, can be displayed by pressing MR.

Follow-up

The memory can also be used to store a number that will be used repeatedly. Children often perform several calculations starting from the same sum of money. They might be working out change from £20.00.

If the 20 is stored in memory it is instantly available each time a new calculation is started, as in the example below:

20 M+ (store £20 in memory)
C (clear the display)
MR ⊟ 14.36 ⊟ (recall the memory and take £14.36 away)
C MR ⊟ 6.78 ⊟ 2.36 ⊟ etc . . .

11. Making sense of errors

Age range
Six to eleven, and teachers.

Group size
Individuals or pairs.

What you need
A calculator.

Background
Calculators can only handle numbers within their design range. Some calculations cannot be done because the numbers are too large or the sum is mathematically impossible.

Entering the following calculation:
999999999 ⊠ 23 ⊟
results in an "overflow error" because the answer is too large to be displayed.

| 22.999997 E | or | E22.999997 |

The display should contain a capital E somewhere to indicate that this error has occurred.

If you are using a scientific calculator the answer will be 2.3^{09}, where the answer is given in exponential form.

Dividing by zero also causes an error because it is mathematically impossible. Keying in the following:
123 ÷ 0 ⊟
should also result in an E for error somewhere in the display. The answer 0 alone is not mathematically acceptable and would be confusing to children.

When purchasing calculators, make sure that the error 'E' is clearly shown in the display and not tucked away so that it is difficult to spot.

12. Other keys

Age range
Ten to eleven, and teachers.

Group size
Pairs or individuals.

What you need
Calculators.

What to do
Most simple calculators have one or two other keys. It is useful to know how they work.

The percentage key %
Although most simple four-function calculators have a percentage key, it is not essential. The way the key operates may vary from one machine to another. It is more helpful for children to learn that 8% can be entered as the decimal fraction 0.08, 75% as 0.75, 115% as 1.15 and so on.

The reciprocal key ¹/x
This key divides the number you enter into one:
2 ¹/x = will give 0.5
Some calculators without a marked reciprocal key do the same thing if you press
2 ÷ =

Change sign keys +/−
This key changes a negative number to positive one and vice versa. It is usually marked as +/−.

2. First steps

This chapter concentrates on specific ideas for encouraging young children to investigate the layout and uses of the calculator.

There are lots of practical ideas for starting children on the road to calculator literacy. The earlier activities give a basic introduction to the layout of the calculator, and can be integrated into ordinary number recognition work and the development of positional language. Reinforcement activities and games have been developed to give valuable practice in an enjoyable way. The section on digital number provides an insight into calculator technology and the formation of numbers. The later activities give practice in keying in number sentences linked to early addition and subtraction activities.

The whole chapter demonstrates the supportive role of the calculator in traditional number activities, and stresses the importance of mental work, which needs to be encouraged at all times.

1. What goes where?

Age range
Five to seven.

Group size
Eight to twelve children.

What you need
Identical calculators for each child, examples or pictures of different types of calculator.

What to do
Note that calculator layouts differ depending on the model and manufacturers. It does not matter which make you use but, to make life easy, it is important to use identical calculators with each group. This allows you to be sure of the responses and to correct errors quickly.

Give each child a calculator. Ask the children to sit in a circle where they can all see your calculator. Ask them to look carefully at it while you point to and name the parts. A diagram of one type of calculator is provided below; the features of most simple calculators are similar though the layout varies. After you have demonstrated, encourage the group to look closely at their own calculators and to point out and name the parts.

Turn this activity into a recall game by pointing to your own calculator and asking the children to name the parts. Vary this by naming the specific parts and asking the children to point to them.

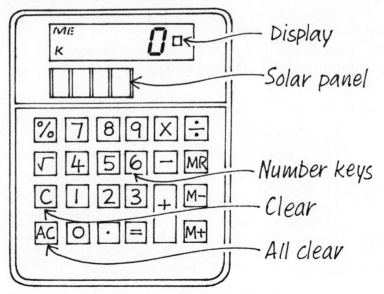

Follow-up

● When the children are familiar with their calculators, prompt them to think about how the calculator works. Where does it get its power from? Do all calculators work in the same way? It would be useful at this point to have other makes and types of calculator available for the children to examine. Failing this, pictures showing different types of calculator would be helpful. The children will discover that calculators use a variety of power sources: mains, batteries and solar power.

● How do we clear the display? A discussion of this is important, as various makes of calculator work in different ways and have different key markings. It is important to know how your chosen model works. The following are examples of key markings which are used to clear the display. The keys work at different levels.

AC clears everything
C clears last entry only
CE clears last entry
ON/C switches the calculator on and clears everything.

You could ask the children to investigate the C/CE key and find out what it does.

● Create a display entitled 'Getting to know your calculator', including samples and pictures of different types of calculator.

2. Simple games

Age range
Five to seven.

Group size
Eight to ten children.

What you need
Identical calculators.

What to do

Game 1: Show me
With a group using identical calculators, ask the children to produce a 1 in their calculator display. They should key in a 1 and turn the calculator round to show you. Next they must clear the display by using the appropriate key.

Initially this can be done in sequence – show me a 1, show me a 2, show me a 3 – until the children become confident with the layout. You can then ask random questions.

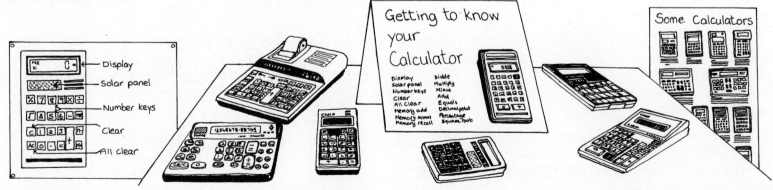

Game 2: Simon says

The rules of the traditional game 'Simon says' need to be established. If Simon says do something, the children do it. If Simon doesn't say, the children ignore the instruction. Then tell the group,

    'Simon says, "Show me a 1".'

    The children must key in a 1 and show you the display. Then continue in a similar fashion.

    'Simon says, "All clear".'

    'Simon says, "Show me a 6".'

    'All clear.'

The children should not carry out the last order as Simon did not say it!

3. Calculator puppet

Age range
Five to seven.

Group size
Two to six children.

What you need
Card, sugar paper, adhesive, scissors, pens, pencils, Blu-Tack, photocopiable page 103.

What to do
Ask the children to design a calculator puppet on A2-size card. The figure could fit in with the school culture or it could be a robot or a clown. The layout of the keypad should be the same as the school's calculators.

The puppet's head can be stuck to the top of the card and the arms and legs can be made from folded sugar paper and glued to the sides of the card.

The children can write the numbers on to the calculator puppet itself or the spaces can be left blank and loose number keys written on separate squares of paper can be attached with Blu-Tack.

If the spaces are left blank, matching games can be played. For example, working in pairs, ask one of the children to choose one of the loose keys and attach it to the puppet in the correct place. The second child can check by looking at the calculator. They then swap roles and continue.

Another activity could be developed by providing the puppet with some of its keys, for example 1, 5 and 9. Ask the children to point to one of the remaining spaces and say which number should go there and why.

Follow-up
A small version of the puppet could be photocopied (see photocopiable page 103) and given to the children, for them to note number key positions, decorate and keep as their personal record.

4. The digital display

Age range
Five to seven.

Group size
Ten to twelve children.

What you need
Identical calculators.

What to do
Ask the children to investigate the display panel of their calculator. How many numbers can they get into the display? Let them try how many ones they can fit in. Is it always eight? Ask them to try with the other digits up to nine.

5. Number patterns

Age range
Five to seven.

Group size
Ten to twelve children.

What you need
Identical calculators, Multilink or Unifix, squared paper, pencils, crayons.

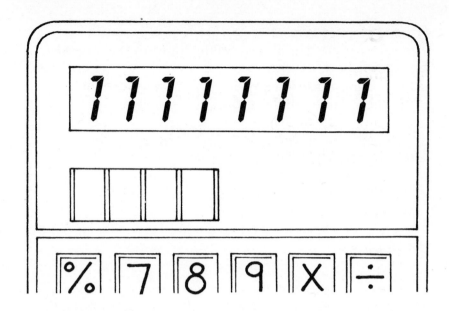

What to do
Ask the children to copy and continue number patterns such as 121212 . . .; 112211 . . .; 131313 . . . They can do this with Multilink or Unifix cubes or beads, and then copy them on the calculator. Then they can record the patterns on squared paper and finally in written form.

Using Multilink/Unifix

Calculator display

Recording on squared paper

Written form

Follow-up
Ask the children to do the same activity in pairs where one child creates a pattern and a second child copies it on his or her calculator.

6. Positional language

Age range
Five to seven.

Group size
Ten to twelve children.

What you need
Identical calculators.

What to do
With the children, look at the layout of the calculator. Identify and name the rows of numbers on the keypad.

Discuss which numbers are on the first row, second row, third row and fourth row.

Follow-up
Ask the children to turn their calculators face down. On which line will they find 0? Let them check their answer. Initially, do this activity in sequence from 0 to 9, then at random.

7. Digital numbers

Age range
Five to seven.

Group size
Six to eight children.

What you need
Identical calculators, squared paper, plain paper, pencils.

What to do
The numbers that appear in the calculator display differ from written numbers. Most children find them fascinating and a comparison between ordinary and digital numbers can prove a useful and interesting line of enquiry.

● Look at the 1 on the calculator display and ask the group how they think it is made up. Can they see the two parts? It is made up of two bars of light rather than one continuous line. Next, look at the number 2. How many bars of light can the children see? Ask them to predict before they look. Encourage them to investigate with other numbers, saying how many bars make up each number.

● Pose open-ended questions and ask the children to investigate which number needs the most bars. Which needs the least? Which numbers have the same number of bars?

The children may need to be encouraged to record their findings. Initially, this may happen in a random way, but it is a good idea to help the children to record their results in a table similar to the one shown below.

	Digital numbers									
	0	1	2	3	4	5	6	7	8	9
Number of → bars	6	2	5	5	4	5	6	4	7	6

8. Building digital numbers

Age range
Five to seven.

Group size
Six to eight children.

What you need
Calculators, lolly sticks or match sticks.

What to do
Let the children construct digital numbers using match sticks, lolly sticks or Unifix cubes. For example, give the children seven lolly sticks. Ask them to key in number 1 on their calculators and then make the digital number with the sticks. Initially, let them do this with numbers taken in order. Then they can try with random numbers.

After the initial investigation, ask the children to predict how many sticks will be needed to make a number and how many will be left over from the seven given. Eventually, they will reason that the number 8 takes the most sticks and that the other numbers are formed from the shape of the 8. If the calculator is tilted to the light, this pattern can usually be seen. When you press 1, only two parts of the number 8 light up.

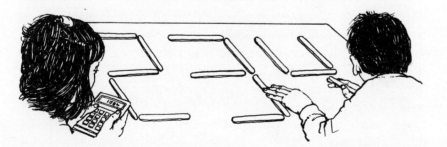

Follow-up
Let the children use seven lolly sticks, plain on one side and coloured on the other, to make a digital layout. Tell them to put the sticks, plain side up, in the shape of the 8.
Ask them to turn over two sticks to represent 1.
They should then turn them back.
Ask them to key in 2 on their calculators.
Tell them to turn over the correct sticks to make a digital 2. Again, the sticks should be turned back when the correct digit has been formed. Encourage the children to continue trying with all the numbers.

9. Using digital paper

Age range
Five to seven.

Group size
Any size.

What you need
Digital activity sheets (see photocopiable pages 104 and 105), strips of card, pencils or felt-tipped pens.

What to do
It is important to point out to the children that digital numbers can be written on special paper, but numbers should not be written in this way in their books.

Using the photocopiable digital paper let the children make the digital numbers 0 to 9 by colouring in the appropriate bars. These can then be cut out and mounted on to folded strips of card to make a concertina digital number book.

Follow-up

For children who are only ready to develop work on numbers 0 to 5, encourage them to create a digital number line using photocopiable page 105. For those who are capable of working with 0 to 9, a similar but extended sheet could be used.

Another way of recording is to make a digital activity book comprising three sheets like those shown below.

Alternatively, digital number activity boards could be made from stiff cards, large enough for children to construct digits with lolly sticks. The children should lay out each digit and find the appropriate number of objects to put in the third columns.

Ask the children to think about where in everyday life, apart from in a calculator display, they can see digital numbers. Can they draw some examples?

0		0	nought
1	•	1	one
2	••	2	two
3	•••	3	three

4	•• ••	4	four
5	••• ••	5	five
6	••• •••	6	six
7	••• ••••	7	seven

8	•••• ••••	8	eight
9	••••• ••••	9	nine
1		2	3	4
5		6	7	8

10. Feely numbers

Age range
Five to seven.

Group size
Two to four children.

What you need
Card, sandpaper, a shallow box, pencils, scissors, adhesive.

What to do
Feely numbers can be made up using the shapes of the bars of digital numbers. Let the children lay a copy of the pattern given on this page on to sheets of sandpaper and trace round them. Several need to be cut out so that they can be arranged to form digital numbers. Each assembled number can be stuck on to a separate piece of card. The children will notice that they feel rough when touched.

Take a shallow box and cut holes in the sides big enough for the children's hands to fit into, as shown. Then place the cards one at a time inside the box so the children can feel but not see them, and let them guess which number they are feeling.

Follow-up
Make a set of ordinary numbers out of sandpaper and ask the children to match them with the sandpaper digital numbers.

11. Numbers are fun!

Age range
Five to seven.

Group size
Pairs.

What you need
Identical calculators, blank cards, digital number strips 0 to 9 (see photocopiable page 106), number cards 0 to 9, two dice, pencils, crayons, a collection of small objects, a tray.

What to do

Activity 1
From a collection of small objects, one child must take a handful and put them on a tray. Then he should count them and key into the calculator the number counted. The second child then checks the count and keys in her total; if the two totals match, the first child scores one point. The children then swap roles. The game continues until each child has had ten turns.

Activity 2
Prepare two sets of cards numbered 0 to 9. The cards should be shuffled and placed face down on a table. The children take turns to pick up a card, turn it over, read the number and key it into the calculator. The other child checks the display. If correct, the first child keeps the card. The children swap roles and the game continues.

Activity 3
Prepare two dice numbered 012345 and 678905. Give each child a copy of the number strip on page 106. The children should take turns choosing a dice, throwing it, and saying the number. Then ask them to key the number shown on the dice into the calculator and colour the number on their digital 0 to 9 number strip. The winner is the child who completes his or her number strip first.

Activity 4
Prepare cards with number statements such as '3 + 9 = 12'. Ask one child to read them out. The other child should key in the statements and check the answers.

Activity 5
Think of a number, for example 9, and say it. Ask the children to add 1 to the number and show the answer on their calculator display.

Alternatively, make a set of cards saying 'add 1' or 'add 2'. Then say a number, and ask each pair to key it into the calculator. Hold up an 'add' card and ask the children to carry out the instructions and key in the addition sum.

Activity 6
Ask the children to key in a number, for example, 10. Key the number into your calculator and then change it by adding another number, to make 12, for instance. Now ask 'What did I add'? Can the children key in a plus sign then a number that will change their display to the same as yours? Ask them what they did. Let them repeat this using different examples.

Activity 7
How many number sentences can the children make

using just the keys 3, 4, 2, 1, ⊞ and ⊟ ? Let them write down all the potential sentences and work out the answers using their calculators.

Activity 8
Children will need to practise keying in addition sums to get the sequence correct. However, they may well be able to do the sums more quickly in their heads. Once the sequence is correct, it is important to establish that it is not necessary to use the calculator to do simple sums; in fact, it takes longer. Games such as 'Beat the calculator' will help to prove this in a fun way.

Working with a pair of children, read out a sum and at the same time key it into your calculator. Ask the children to call out the answer. The person who gives the correct response first is the winner. Using simple examples, the children will usually be able to do the sums and will realise that mental work is better for smaller numbers and that keying in takes more time.

3. Moving into number

Having grasped the layout of a calculator and how to key in numbers, children can use their calculators to support the development of their early number skills.

This chapter gives an insight into activities which integrate the calculator into the mathematics curriculum alongside other aids to develop children's fascination with numbers.

Addition, subtraction, multiplication and division can all be developed through games. Strategies for using the constant function, investigational work and number lines are also highlighted. Mental work should be encouraged at all times when these activities are being developed. Children need to estimate first with mental methods in order to be sure that their calculator is giving them a reasonable answer.

1. Finish the sentence

Age range
Six to eight.

Group size
Pairs.

What you need
Photocopiable pages 107, 108 and 109, scissors, counters, calculators.

What to do
First make number cards by cutting up the photocopiable sheet on page 107. These will be used for answer cards. It may be useful to photocopy these on a coloured paper to distinguish them from the digital set. Next, photocopy and cut out the digital numbers, addition and subtraction signs (see page 108). Copy the baseboard photocopiable sheet on page 109.

The aim of the game is to correctly predict the numbers and sign needed to complete the number sentence correctly. The number pack should be shuffled and placed face down on the table. Ask the first child to take the digital cards, shuffle them, turn up the first one and place it in the first circle on the baseboard. Then she should choose one card from the number pack. This card should then be placed face up in the answer circle. The second child must choose the appropriate sign card and predict what the missing number must be for the number sentence to be completed correctly. The children should then key the sentence into the calculator. If it is correct, the child who predicted takes a counter from the pile.

The children then swap roles. The winner is the one with the most counters after 15 goes.

2. Win a bone

Age range
Six to eight.

Group size
Pairs.

What you need
Photocopiable page 110, coloured pencils, calculators.

What to do

Give each pair a copy of the baseboard for 'Win a Bone' (see page 110). Explain that the object of the game is to win as many bones as possible for their pet dog. Ask each player to choose one of the dogs shown at the bottom of the baseboard, colour it in with her chosen colour and write her name in the name tag.

The players must take turns to choose a sum dog. Ask them to read the incomplete number sentence which is written on the dog's coat. The first child should predict the missing number and say it out loud. Both children must then check the sentence using the calculator.

If it is correct, the child who made the prediction colours the bone with his chosen colour and fills in the number sentence. The children then swap roles.

If the answer was incorrect, the other player must choose a sum dog and try to predict the answer to the new number sentence. The winner is the child who has coloured the most bones at the end of the game.

3. Snakes

Age range
Five to seven.

Group size
Pairs.

What you need
Counters, photocopiable page 111, calculators, Unifix or Multilink cubes.

What to do
Give each pair a photocopy of page 111. There are four snakes and the children can play two games on each sheet.

Let the children begin by choosing a snake from game one and placing their counter on the first number on its tail. The children take turns to move along their own snake. Each move begins with the player keying into the calculator the number on which their counter is placed. To move up the body of the snake, the player must add a number to the one shown in the calculator display which will make it up to the number shown at the top of the snake's hump. For example, $3 + \square = 6$ becomes $3 + 3 = 6$.

If the answer is correct, the player can move along to the next number. An incorrect answer means that the player has to wait and try again. Both children must check the result with the calculator. To move on to the next number, going down the snake, a number has to be subtracted. The winner is the first player to land on his or her snake's head. Some children may benefit from using Multilink or Unifix cubes during the game.

Follow-up

Once the children understand the rules of the game, they might like to design their own games based on the same idea. The games then can be tried by different pairs of children.

4. Total

Age range

Six to eight.

Group size

Pairs.

What you need

Number cards 1 to 7, calculators, coins.

What to do

Each pair should toss a coin to decide who starts. One child must then spread out the digit cards face up on a table.

Ask one child to choose any digit between 1 and 7 and pick up the corresponding number card. He should then enter it into the calculator display. The second child then has to pick up another card and add its number to that shown in the calculator display. The first player then chooses another card and adds that digit to the running total. The number cards can each be used only once in each game. The game continues until one player either reaches 21 or forces her partner to push the running total over 21. For example:

- Child A: 1
- Child B: 2
- Child A: 3
- Child B: 4
- Child A: 5
- Child B: 6

The total is 21, so child B wins.

- Child A: 6
- Child B: 2
- Child A: 7
- Child B: 3
- Child A: 1
- Child B: 4

The total is over 21, so child A wins.

Follow-up

Ask the children to try to explain the strategies they used to win the game.

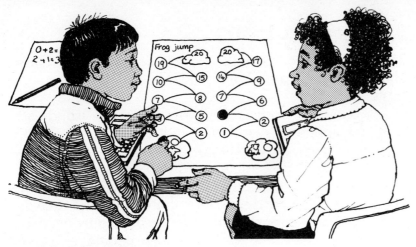

5. Frog jumps

Age range
Five to seven.

Group size
Pairs.

What you need
Photocopiable page 112, counters, calculators, pencils.

What to do
The object of the game is to move the frogs on photocopiable page 112 from the lily-pads to the rocks by moving along the tracks of stepping stones. Prepare the sheets by filling in numbers to the children's needs, as shown in the example on this page. Let each player choose a frog and place a coloured counter on the first stone on his track. The children should key their starting numbers into their calculators.

Taking turns, the players have to predict which number should be added to reach the number on the second stepping stone. The prediction must be keyed into their calculators, for example.

$$0 \boxplus 2 \boxminus 2$$

If they are right, the counters move on to the next stone. This new number is kept in the calculator until the next go. If either child is wrong, he or she has to miss a turn and must clear the calculator and key in the number on the stone where he or she is stuck. The winner is the first child to reach the rock.

Follow-up
You can adapt the game by mixing addition and subtraction and using numbers greater than 20. Vary the tracks by using different contexts, for example, dogs trying to find a bone, or treasure hunts.

The children can also be encouraged to record their calculations on paper. This will help them to explain the game while it is in progress, and it will provide a diagnostic tool to help you assess the children's activities.

6. Match it

Age range
Six to eight.

Group size
Pairs.

What you need
Counters, crayons, calculators, photocopiable page 113.

What to do

Give each pair a photocopied sheet and let each player choose one side of the egg. The first player should place a counter on a chosen number on his side of the egg. He then places a second counter on the number sentence which he believes adds up to the number he has just selected. For example, if the first player places a counter on 20, he places another one on the number sentence '18 + 2'.

The second player then checks this using the calculator. If the number sentence is correct, that section of the egg can be coloured by the first child. The first player to colour in his or her half of the egg is the winner.

Follow-up

You can adapt this activity in two ways. The design of the picture can be linked with topic work, for example, a face, and you can change the number sentences to suit your children's abilities.

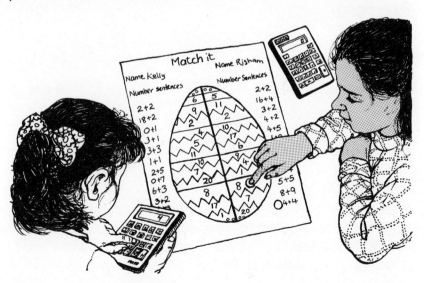

7. Missing keys

Age range
Six to nine.

Group size
Pairs or individuals.

What you need
Calculators, prepared sheets (see below), pencils.

What to do

Give the children practice in estimating and checking by preparing sheets of number sentences with something missing! In the first examples below, the answer is given but the operation ($+$, $-$, $\times$, $\div$) has been left out. In the second example, numbers have been omitted.

Example 1
4 □ 3 = 1
4 □ 3 = 7
4 □ 3 =12
20 □ 10 = 2
7 □ 10 = 17
12 □ 2 = 24

Example 2
3 + □ = 5
2 + □ = 12
□ − 4 = 10

Devise some similar examples and ask the children to predict what is missing. Then they can check using the calculator. Ensure that the sheets you make suit the ability of the children.

8. Daisy chain

Age range
Six to nine.

Group size
Any.

What you need
Calculators, daisy chain sheets (see below).

What to do
Design some number sheets similar to the example below using numbers suitable for your children's abilities. Give each child a sheet and ask them to look at the heart of the daisy, which tells them which multiplication story they are dealing with. In the example shown, the first daisy is ×2. They must read the petals in turn and key in the number sentence, for example, 2 ⊠ 2 ⊟ 4. Ask them to write the answer in the outer petal. Let them continue until the whole flower is completed.

Follow-up
This activity can also be carried out by keying in the constant function for a particular number.

Using the first example, ask the children to enter 2 ⊠ ⊠ ⊟ 0, and then enter the petal numbers. Encourage the children to predict the answer before pressing the equals sign.

Speed games can be played by pairs of children to develop mental arithmetic. One child can say the number sentence and predict the answer, while the other child simultaneously keys in the sentence and reads the answer. Can the calculator be beaten? The children will soon learn when it is better to use the calculator and when it is quicker to use their heads.

9. Division darts

Age range
Six to nine.

Group size
Pairs or individuals.

What you need
Examples of 'division darts' sheets, calculators, pencils.

What to do
Prepare some 'division darts' sheets like those shown here. Ask the children to look at the centre of the dartboard to identify the number by which they are dividing. They should then divide the numbers on the

middle ring by that number, predicting the answer and checking using the calculator. Finally they should record the number in the outer ring.

Follow-up

The children can modify the game by using the constant function, for example, 2 ⊞ ⊞ ⊟ 0, then keying in the number on the middle ring, predicting the answer then pressing the ⊟ key to bring up the answer.

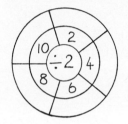 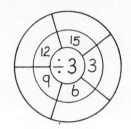 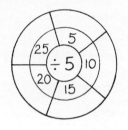

10. Four in a row

Age range

Seven to eleven.

Group size

Three to four children.

What you need

Calculators, counters, number grid sheets.

What to do

Prepare a set of grids with appropriate numbers depending on the area of number work you want the children to practise. The grids should contain the answers to all the possible sums that can be made with the numbers and signs in the choice panel.

Below are examples for addition and subtraction.

Ask the children to choose a combination of two numbers from the choice panel and, depending on the sign given, carry out that operation, predicting the answer and then checking using the calculator. If the children are correct, they should place a coloured counter over the answer number on the grid. The children should take turns to do this and the winner is the player with four counters in a row in any direction.

Follow-up

This type of game can be modified in many ways. You can simplify it so that the children just have to get two or three in a row, and the numbers can be simplified to suit the children's abilities. You can also use all four number operations in the game.

Example 1

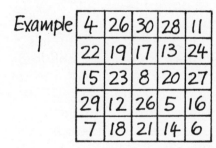

Choice panel

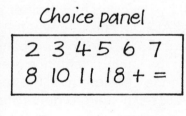

Example 2

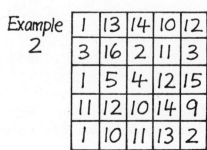

Choice panel

20 19 18 17 15 9

8 7 5 4 3 — =

11. Number pattern squares

Age range
Seven to nine.

Group size
Six to ten children.

What you need
Photocopiable page 114, calculators, pencils, crayons, Centicubes.

What to do
Talk to the children about the number pattern 2, 4, 6. What comes next? Why? What are they adding each time? How could they show this with Centicubes on the 100 square on photocopiable page 114? Could they do it by covering every other number with a cube?

Ask the children whether it is possible to obtain this pattern of 2 from their calculators. Remind the children of the special sentence they put into the calculator to set up the constant function for 2, for example, 2 ⊞ ⊞ ⊟ 0. Ask each child to generate the pattern of 2 on the calculator and colour the pattern on a 100 square. Can they describe what is happening?

Follow-up
This idea can be used with other numbers such as 3, 5 and 10, and the pattern developed. It is also possible to develop this as a prediction game. Given the pattern of 3, ask the children to predict the pattern and mark it on the 100 square with Centicubes. They can then use the constant function of + 3 to check the answers. If they are correct, they can colour in the squares.

Some numbers are common to more than one pattern. Using a 100 square, ask the children to generate the pattern of 3 and cover the squares with blue cubes. Then ask them to record the pattern for 6 with yellow cubes. If two cubes need to go on to one square, they must fix one on top of the other. What do they notice? Do some numbers have two cubes? Why has this happened?

12. Multiples galore

Age range
Seven to nine.

Group size
Individuals or small groups.

What you need
Calculators, number grid sheets, pencils.

What to do
Make copies of a number grid sheet for the children. The number grid shown here is based on the × 2 constant, so all the numbers are multiples of 2.

Remind the children how to set their calculators to the constant you are using: in the case of × 2, 2 ⊠ ⊠ ⊟ 0.

Let the children take turns to choose a target number from the number square. The first child, having chosen, must enter a number into her calculator which she thinks will give the target number when applied to the constant function; in this case, when multiplied by 2. For instance, if a child chooses 20, he or she should predict that 10 is the number needed to be put into the calculator. This should then be keyed in and the ⊟ pressed to display 20. As the child was correct, he or she must cover number 20 with a coloured counter. The winner is the first child to cover three numbers in a row in any direction.

Follow-up

The constant can be changed for any number and any sign can be used. Select the numbers in the grids carefully to match the constant pattern being generated.

Other variations could be to make the number of correct answers in a row more demanding, say four in a row, or even five in a row, in any direction.

When the children understand the game strategies, ask them to construct their own number grid for their friends to solve. They should link it to a particular number and sign.

13. Number lines

Age range

Seven to eleven.

Group size

Individuals or pairs.

What you need

Number lines from 0 to 20, calculators, photocopiable page 115, Unifix or Multilink cubes.

6	18	24	36
2	16	10	12
8	14	4	32
18	22	28	20
26	30	24	3

What to do

Give each child a number strip sheet from 0 to 20. Ask the children to count on in twos starting at 0 (0, 2, 4, 6 . . .) and to place Unifix cubes on these numbers. Can they produce this pattern on the calculator? What number sentence would they need to use?

Can the children describe this pattern? By how many does it grow each time? Do they notice anything about these numbers? Have they a special name?

Now ask the group to use their number lines and, starting at 1, count on in twos, placing the Unifix cubes on the correct numbers (1, 3, 5, 7 . . .). What number sequence do they get this time? Do these numbers have a special name? Do the children know why they are called 'odd' numbers?

Now ask the children to investigate how they can get the calculator to generate the odd number pattern starting at 1. They should eventually realise that 2 ⊞ ⊞ ⊟ 1 will start the pattern at 1.

Follow-up

Ask the children to think about where they see odd and even numbers in everyday life. Give them copies of page 115 to develop the idea of street numbers.

4. Place value

Children's success in the computational aspects of mathematics depends heavily on their understanding of place value.

If children have only a tenuous grasp of place value, their ability to handle numbers will be reduced. This applies not only to the traditional algorithms for the four rules of number, but to non-standard ways of recording these processes, and to the general ability to deal with numbers and investigate patterns and relationships.

The calculator can be regarded as an embodiment of the tens number system. It has been programmed to respond correctly to all the rules of place value. As such, it can be used in a wide range of activities to assist and develop children's understanding of place value.

However, the calculator does not make other structural apparatus redundant. Multilink, Centicubes, Diennes apparatus, abacuses and Cuisennaire rods will continue to have a valuable role in developing this vital understanding.

The activities in this chapter will help to increase the understanding of place value. They will also help teachers to diagnose and pin-point difficulties and misunderstandings.

In general, the activities deal with small whole numbers. However, many can be extended to highlight similar concepts using larger numbers and those which contain decimal fractions.

Eighty-three	83
Forty-six	46
Ninety	90
Eighteen	18
Thirty-seven	307
Fifty-nine	59
Check number: 333	603

1. Reading numbers

Age range
Five to eleven, depending upon the examples.

Group size
Pairs.

What you need
One calculator between two, prepared activity sheets, pencils.

What to do
Give each pair of children a prepared sheet with several sets of numbers similar to the ones shown below. Provide a 'check answer' as here, which is the sum of the numbers in the list. For example:
- Eighty-three
- Forty-six
- Ninety
- Eighteen
- Thirty-seven
- Fifty-nine

Check answer: 333

Ask the first child in each pair to read out the numbers while the other child writes them down in figures, either on a separate sheet or on the one provided.

The reader should then key the written numbers into the calculator, pressing the ⊞ key after each new number to give a running total. Point out to young children that repeated additions can be made without pressing the ⊟ key after each number is added.

After the last number has been entered, the children should press the ⊟ key to obtain the final total. If the numbers have been read and then keyed in correctly, the answer in the display should be the same as the check answer given. If the answers do not agree, the children can swap roles and repeat the set to make sure there were no reading or keying errors.

If you ask the children to estimate the total before doing the addition, this will encourage accuracy and give you information about their concepts of number. Let the children swap roles for the next set of numbers.

Each set of numbers should be completed in full before moving on so that any difficulties can be sorted out. Writing the numbers down is a vital part of this activity as it means you can identify where the problems have arisen. Remind the children to use the AC key before starting on the next set of numbers.

Follow-up

This activity can be used with children of any age and the numbers can be varied according to their ability; for example, the following list might be suitable for older or more able children.

- Two thousand three hundred and seventy-six

- One thousand four hundred and eighteen

- Four thousand nine hundred and twenty-seven

- Three thousand six hundred and twenty-four

Check answer: 12345

2. Nothing left

Age range
Six upwards, depending on the numbers selected.

Group size
Individuals or pairs.

What you need
Calculators, prepared activity sheets, pencils.

What to do
Give children a copy of a prepared activity sheet with number routes similar to those below, and ask them to find out what must be subtracted at each stage to get the number further down the route to zero. They must make the new number shown by subtracting a single number each time.

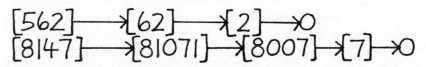

Encourage the children to work out new routes for other children to use.

Follow-up
Extend the activity to include numbers with decimal fractions. For example:

$$[45.23] \longrightarrow [40.23] \longrightarrow [40.03] \longrightarrow [40] \longrightarrow 0$$

Reverse the activity by asking children to add numbers to reach a new number.

3. Place invaders

Age range
Seven upwards.

Group size
Individuals.

What you need
Calculators, prepared playing sheets (see photocopiable page 116), a set of starting numbers.

What to do
This is a game version of 'Nothing left'. The aim of the game is to reduce the given number to zero by subtracting numbers from the different place value columns, one at a time. Start with three-digit numbers, and the number subtracted should reduce a single column to zero each time. For example, with a starting number of 362, it can be reduced to zero by subtracting 2 (from the units column), then 60 (from the tens column) and then 300 (from the hundreds column).

If a child makes a mistake, either by subtracting the wrong number, or by a keying error, he or she must continue with the number that is left in the display. If the display becomes full of digits through a mistake, the original number should be keyed in again.

Young children might like to keep a tally of the number of goes taken to reduce each number to zero. For older children, a simple scoring system can be used where each new starting number gives 100 points. Each go at reducing the number to zero takes away ten points. Accidents and mistakes have to be paid for in points!

Follow-up
The game can be played at various levels and can be returned to many times as the pupils' ability grows.
- Use a three-digit start number and reduce the digits to 0 in any order.
- Use a three-digit start number and reduce the digits in descending or ascending order.
- Use a four-digit or larger start number and reduce the digits in ascending or descending order.
- Use a three-digit start number but play using addition. The start number must be increased to make exactly 1000.
- Use four-, five- or six-digit numbers, and add numbers until the number of zeros equals the number of starting digits. For example, 1234 has to be increased to 10000, 12345 has to be increased to 100000, and 123456 to 1000000.
- Include numbers with decimal fractions such as 456.32, which have to be reduced to zero by subtraction.

4. Please may I have . . .?

Age range
Seven upwards, depending on the numbers used.

Group size
Pairs.

What you need
Two calculators for each pair.

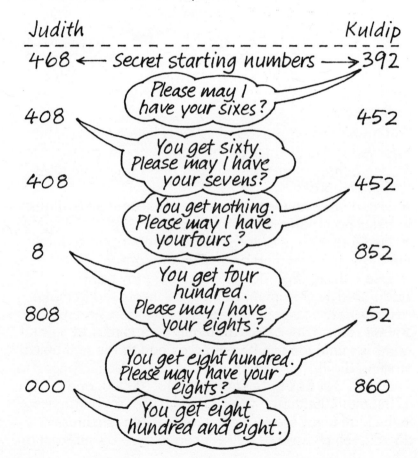

What to do
Ask each player to key a secret starting number into the calculator. The numbers must all have an agreed number of digits.

The players should take it in turns to ask each other for their numbers, one digit at a time. If Kuldip asks for the number 6, Judith, who started with 468, would have to give him the value of the 6 in that number (60). She subtracts it from her total and Kuldip adds it to his total. Judith would then have 408 left and Kuldip, who started with 392, would have 452. Play then passes to Judith, who asks Kuldip for a number.

If, as the game progresses, a player has two of a particular digit in her number, she must give both. If a player doesn't have the digit asked for, her opponent gets nothing. The winner is the first player who makes his calculator show a number with one more digit than the starting number. For instance, with a two-digit starting number, the winner needs over 100, and with a three-digit starting number, the winner needs over 1000. If, as in the example shown, neither player can reach 1000, the loser is the first player to be reduced to zero.

With some calculators, the operator sign is shown in the display. In this case, the children can show each other their displays before pressing the ⊟ key. This will enable them to check that the correct numbers are being added and subtracted, and that the right operator is being used. Once checked, the ⊟ key can be pressed and the new number secretly displayed.

The choice of starting numbers can be crucial; too big and you can lose in the first go, too small and you can never win. Although there is an element of luck involved, there are opportunities to develop interesting strategies for selecting a good starting number, and keeping track of the numbers requested.

Follow-up

The game can be extended to use larger numbers. Up to eight digits can be entered into the calculator. With an eight-digit starting number, the winner will be the player with an overflow error!

Older children will find it quite a challenge to use the game with decimal fractions. If starting numbers are less than 1, the winner is the first to obtain a number greater than 1. You can stipulate how many decimal places the children should use.

5. Count on

Age range

Five to eleven, depending on the numbers chosen.

Group size

Individuals or pairs.

What you need

One calculator between two.

What to do

For this activity, children need to set up a constant function of 'add 1'. You may need to do this for very young children, until they become more proficient.

Once the constant function has been set up, children can simply use the calculator as a counting device with the display showing the changing numbers.

It is important that the children realise when the display changes to include another place value position; for instance from 9 to 10, or 99 to 100.

> **A Constant Reminder**
>
> **Method 1**
> Start number $-$ Constant $=$ $=$ $=$
>
> **Method 2**
> Constant $-$ $-$ Start number $=$ $=$ $=$
>
> **Universal Method**
> Constant $-$ $-$ $=$ ◯ Start number $=$ $=$ $=$

The calculator allows children to see the effect of adding an extra 1 to 99. They can repeat the exercise many times.

Children can also count backwards by setting up a subtraction constant. To subtract 1, the following keys must be pressed:

- Method one: 1 $-$ $-$ (start number) $=$ $=$ $=$
- Method two: (start number) $-$ 1 $=$ $=$ $=$

With method two, children can change from addition to subtraction constants with the last number in the display as the starting point.

For example:

Press: 97 $+$ 1 $=$ $=$ $=$ $=$ $-$ 1 $=$ $=$ $=$
Display: 98 99 100 101   100 99 98

Follow-up

You can also set up the calculator so that children can count in tens from any starting point. This can be helpful in investigating the pattern made when adding 10.

10 $+$ $+$ 34 $=$ $=$ $=$ $=$ $=$
      44 54 64 74 84

The multiplication and division constants can be used in the same way to show the effect of multiplying and dividing by multiples of 10.

6. Box numbers

Age range
Seven upwards, depending on the examples used.

Group size
Individuals or pairs.

What you need
Calculators, prepared activity sheets, pencils.

What to do
Give the children prepared worksheets with examples like those shown below. The children can use only the given set of digits to make the numbers shown in the target answers. In some instances, the targets will be open-ended, such as 'make the smallest number'; in others, the target will be more precise.

Children can use the calculator to try many examples easily and accurately. They can also look for patterns and try new ideas.

Examples
Try to make the following target numbers. Use the digits 1, 2, 3 and 4. You must use each digit once for each question.

- [   ] [   ] + [   ] [   ] Make the biggest possible answer.

- [   ] [   ] × [   ] [   ] Make the answer 448.

- [   ] [   ] + [   ] [   ] Make the answer 37.

In these examples, children must understand the importance of placing the largest digits in the tens positions to make a large number, and the smallest digits in the tens positions to make a small number. In this type of activity, children should record their work as they go along. Some choices give similar answers and careful recording is required to select the right combinations. Encourage discussion about the strategies used.

7. Shift it

Age range
Eight upwards.

Group size
Individuals, pairs or groups.

What you need
One calculator between two.

What to do
Give the children a single unit digit. Ask them to key this into the calculator. Then ask them what they must do to move that number into the tens position.

They are not allowed to add or subtract numbers, but must multiply and divide to shift the number. Once there, you could ask them to move it back to the units position or on to the hundreds position.

Start number	shift it to	Key presses
6	Tens	6 ☒ 10 ▣
60	Units	60 ÷ 10 ▣
6	Hundreds	6 ☒ 100 ▣

Initially, the children might take several goes to move the number, but as their understanding grows, encourage them to make the shift in a single jump.

Encourage the children to write down their key presses before they make them. The results will be a useful diagnostic aid and can be used to discuss the process.

Follow-up

The start numbers could be larger than single units, so that the children have to shift the number more than one position.

For more able or older children, include decimal fractions in the start number, or ask them to shift the numbers into a decimal fraction position. For example, ask them to shift the number 6 into the hundredths position.

8. Add 10

Age range
Five upwards.

Group size
Individuals or pairs.

What you need
One calculator between two.

What to do
Ask the children to set up their calculator with an add 10 constant. When they have done this, ask them to enter the numbers below and to press ▣ after each number. They should write down the new number.

- 13 ▣
- 19 ▣
- 24 ▣
- 40 ▣
- 33 ▣

Encourage the children to look carefully at their numbers. Can they see a pattern? What has happened to the units digit? What has happened to the tens digit? Can they work out the answers to some more questions like these without using the calculator?

> ### A Constant Reminder
> ### Universal Method
>
> Constant ⊞ ⊞ ▣ ○ start number ▣ ▣ ▣

9. Forecast and check

Age range
Six upwards.

Group size
Individuals or pairs.

What you need
Calculators, pencils, prepared worksheets.

What to do
This activity requires children to forecast the answer to a problem and then to check their answer using the calculator. It is a useful follow-up to the 'Add 10' activity (see page 47).

Create a worksheet with simple examples like those shown below.

The calculator gives the children an immediate feedback to their forecast. It also enables a large number of examples to be tackled easily and the resulting pattern to be identified.

Number Operation	Forecast	Check
95 + 10	105	✓
191 + 10	192	✗ 201
292 + 10	293	✗ 302
999 + 10		

Vary the activity, depending on the age and ability of the children.
● Don't ask them to forecast initially, but use the answers generated by the calculator to help them spot a particular pattern and make a general rule (see 'Add 10', page 47). This is useful when working with young children or when introducing a new concept.
● When the children are familiar with this, ask them to forecast each individual question and then use the calculator to check their answers.
● Then ask them to forecast a whole set of questions, and only use the calculator to check when all the questions have been completed.

Follow-up
Make up some more complicated examples involving place value skills and understanding. You could ask the children to predict the answers to questions such as:
● 400 − 1
● 107 − 10
● 79 + 10
● 146 + 100
● 14 × 10
● 14 × 100
● 140 ÷ 10
● 1700 ÷ 100

10. Follow the track

Age range
Eight upwards depending on the numbers used.

Group size
Pairs.

What you need
One calculator for each pair, photocopiable page 117.

What to do
Give the pairs a number track like the one shown, using page 117. The track shows only the numbers left after the operation has been performed. Each of the operations in the example shown here involves whole numbers in multiples of 10.

Ask the children to enter the start number into their calculators. They should then enter the operation and the number they think will produce the next number on the track.

The calculator enables children to experiment with different numbers easily and with confidence.

Follow-up
When they are familiar with the idea, ask the children to make up their own tracks. Give them a photocopy of page 117. The tracks they make could be for younger pupils, using smaller numbers, or for other pupils in the same class. Invite the children to make up a collection of tracks to use when they have a few spare moments.

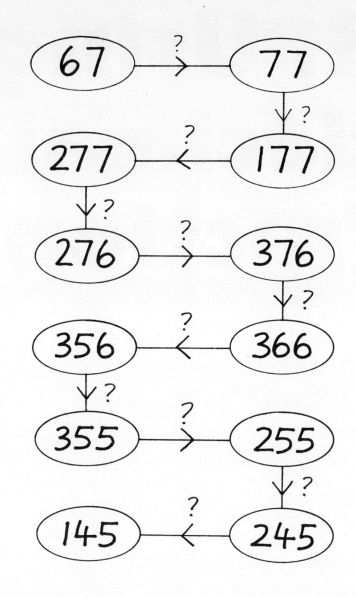

Check with your calculator

5. Using decimal fractions

When children are allowed to use calculators freely they will soon find the screen displaying numbers containing decimal fractions. Young children may accidentally press the ÷ key instead of the − key and find an answer containing decimals. The √ key or % key will also produce answers which may fill the whole display and leave children bewildered.

This raises two questions. The first is how best to prepare young children to understand decimal fractions. Teachers need to realise that children will be aware of them earlier than has previously been the case, and that they will crop up at unexpected moments.

The second question is how we can help children make sense of numbers containing many places of decimals which have no real meaning or relevance to the calculations they are doing. Sharing sweets amongst friends might well involve half or even quarters of sweets, but when seating children on coaches for a school trip, it is impossible to deal in anything less than whole children!

This chapter aims to suggest some answers to both these questions.

1. Shopping sums

Age range
Six upwards.

Group size
Pairs.

What you need
A class shop or priced objects (some in pence, some in pounds), one calculator between two.

What to do
A child's first introduction to decimals is often associated with money. Some amounts of money are written as pence and others as pounds. Ask children to add mixtures of the two with a calculator and they will come up with some interesting answers!

Make up some shopping sums, either using a class shop or a list of prices. For example, you could ask the children to add up the following prices:
- Comic   23p
- Book   £1.95
- Pen   39p
- Record   £2.33

Give each pair a calculator to do the additions. Make sure that they discuss their answers to see whether they are likely to be right. Some are bound to obtain £66.28 by keying in the pence as pounds. Use their answers to discuss the importance of the decimal point in separating whole pounds from parts of pounds.

Ask them to check their answer with their partner or with other pairs.

In the above example, when entered correctly, the final result shown on the display will be 4.9 – missing the final zero. The calculator automatically removes a zero in this position. It is important to explain this to young children so that they know how to interpret it in a money context.

2. Left-overs

Age range
Seven upwards.

Group size
Individuals or small groups.

What you need
One calculator between two, 100 real or plastic pennies.

What to do
When children are involved in sharing activities there are often left-overs at the end. The calculator will record these left-overs as decimal fractions. Children need to understand how these decimal fractions relate to the actual sharing activity.

Ask the children to investigate the sharing of a pound (100p) between different numbers of children. They may start with two, then three and so on. Initially children should share out the coins, putting aside any left-over pence. When they have done the sharing, ask them to repeat the exercise using the calculator and to record their answers.

People	Share	Left	Calculator
2	50p	0p	50
3	33p	1p	33.333333
4	25p	0p	25
5	20p	0p	20
6	16p	4p	16.666666
7	14p	2p	14.285714

Let the children look at the divisions that do not work out exactly. They should explore the link between having pennies left over and a calculator display showing a decimal fraction. When sharing by three, for example, ask:

- How many pence does each child get?
- Why does the calculator show more than 33p?
- What does the calculator answer mean?
- Point out that the answer lies between 33 and 34.

For other examples, you need to discuss all the extra digits. Compare the calculator answer to the sharing of the pennies and show them that they still only receive the same number of whole pence. The rest tells them how much more they would receive if they could split what is left over. When dealing with pounds, they only need to be concerned with the first two digits after the decimal point; with pence only the first decimal place is important.

Follow-up
Let the children do the same activity by sharing a packet of biscuits or sweets between different numbers of children.

3. Decimal fractions

Age range
Nine upwards.

Group size
Pairs or small groups.

What you need
Pencils, paper, calculators, newspapers or magazines.

What to do
Begin by asking the children to look at simple fractions for which they may already know the decimal equivalent, such as a half or quarter. This could be done by asking them how we make 0.5 from ½. Ask them to try it out on their calculators. They could also look for examples of decimal fractions in newspapers and magazines.

To change common fractions to decimal fractions, you may need to show the children how to use the ⊟ key. For example:

- For ¼ we key in 1 ⊟ 4 ⊟ 0.25
- For ¾ we key in 3 ⊟ 4 ⊟ 0.75

When children are confident in doing this, ask them to use a calculator to find the decimal equivalents of these fractions: ½, ¼, ²⁄₄, ¾, ⅛, ²⁄₈, ³⁄₈, ⁴⁄₈.

Let the children extend this pattern and see if they can discover how it changes.

4. Equivalent fractions

Age range
Nine upwards.

Group size
Pairs or small groups.

What you need
Paper, pencils, calculators.

What to do
Ask children to use their calculators to change the following fractions into decimal fractions: ⅕; ²⁄₅; ³⁄₅; ⁴⁄₅; ⁵⁄₅; ¹⁄₁₀; ²⁄₁₀; ³⁄₁₀; ⁴⁄₁₀; ⁵⁄₁₀; ⁶⁄₁₀; ⁷⁄₁₀; ⁸⁄₁₀; ⁹⁄₁₀; ¹⁰⁄₁₀.

Ask them if they can spot any common fractions which have the same decimal fractions. These are called equivalent fractions. Invite the children to write down any pairs which are the same.

Follow-up
Ask the children to find some more equivalent fractions for any of the decimal fractions they have made. Encourage them to try different starting points. What other fractions, for example, give the same decimal fractions as ½? Children will enjoy building these patterns and looking for the rules about maintaining equivalence.

0.25 0.75 0.375 0.1 0.4

5. Decimal number lines

Age range
Seven upwards.

Group size
Pairs or small groups.

What you need
Prepared number line sheets, pencils, calculators.

What to do
Give the children number line sheets like the one below, and ask them to work out the numbers marked with capital letters and write them down. They should then add the numbers using a calculator. They must check the calculator total by comparing it with the check answer given.

Number line

Check answer = 1·7

Follow-up
The same idea can be extended to include hundredths.

Number line

Check answer = 8·18

6. Decimal sandwiches

Age range
Ten upwards.

Group size
Individuals or pairs.

What you need
Prepared worksheets, pencils, calculators.

What to do
Prepare some worksheets on which a decimal number on the number line is squashed between two other decimals. Its approximate position should be shown by an arrow. Ask the children to put the given digits into the right order to show the value of the decimal fraction.

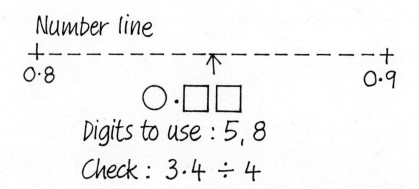

Number line

Digits to use : 5, 8

Check : 3·4 ÷ 4

Encourage them to look closely at the number line to discover the range of the line and the approximate value at the position of the arrow.
Once they have worked out the correct digits, they

should complete the check sum on a calculator to give the correct placing of the decimal digits.

Follow-up
Children will enjoy making up their own examples, using a calculator to work out the check sum required to give the correct answer.

7. Box numbers

Age range
Ten upwards.

Group size
Pairs or small groups.

What you need
Prepared worksheets, pencils, calculators.

What to do
Prepare worksheets with puzzles showing fractions and their decimal equivalents. The children should fit the given digits into the brackets to make a matching fraction and decimal pair. They should test the result using a calculator. You could use examples such as these:

- $\dfrac{[\ \ ]}{[\ \ ]} = 0 \cdot [\ \ ]\ [\ \ ]$

Digits to use: 3, 4, 5, 7.

- $\dfrac{[\ \ ]}{[\ \ ]} = [\ \ ] \cdot [\ \ ]$

Digits to use: 1, 5, 8, 9.

8. Squeeze

Age range
Ten upwards.

Group size
Pairs.

What you need
Coloured pencils, one calculator between two, number lines drawn on graph paper (tenth divisions are useful).

What to do
The aim of the game is for one of the players to get three of their marks in a row on the number line. At the same time, players must try to stop their opponents from doing the same.

In the easiest games, the number line should be divided into tenths, between 0 and 1.

$$+-+-+-+-+-+-+-+-+-+-+$$
0   0·5   1·0

Playing numbers
1 2 3 4 5 6 7 8 9 10 11 12

Ask each player to take turns to choose two numbers from the playing numbers. These should be made into a fraction which is then converted to a decimal fraction using the calculator.

The player must mark the correct position of the decimal fraction on the number line. Players should use different coloured pencils to mark their points. If the decimal equivalent of any fraction is greater than one, the mark goes off the line and that player misses a go.

Sample of play
Player 1 takes 1 and   4 to give 0.25;
Player 2 takes 6 and 10 to give 0.6;
Player 1 takes 2 and   3 to give 0.6666666;
Player 2 takes 2 and   5 to give 0.4;
Player 1 takes 1 and   3 to give 0.3333333;
Player 2 takes 3 and   8 to give 0.375;
Player 1 takes 4 and 11 to give 0.3636363 and wins.

Follow-up
Many of the fractions will be greater than two decimal places and this can introduce work on rounding decimal fractions to one, two or three decimal places, according to the level of the players.

9. Bull's-eye

Age range
Ten upwards.

Group size
Individuals, small groups or the whole class.

What you need
Calculators, pencils, paper.

What to do
Give each child a calculator, a target number and a starting number. Explain that the aim of the game is to find out what number they need to multiply the start number by to get as close as possible to the target number. The game will help to extend children's understanding of the decreasing value and influence of the digits to the right of the decimal point. For example, with a target number of 100 and a starting number of 23, one might make the following guesses:

Guess	Answer	Too big	Too small
× 6	138		
× 4	92		
× 5	115		
× 4.5	103.5		
× 4.4	101.2		
× 4.3	98.9		
× 4.35	100.05		

It is essential that the children record their play as they go along, since it soon becomes impossible to remember which numbers have been tried and which answers obtained.

Follow-up
The game can be a useful reinforcement or introduction to larger numbers and can help children develop trial and improvement strategies to find, for example, how many 7s there are in 3456. It is also a good introduction to decimal fractions. Children soon realise that they may need a number between two numbers. They may begin with a half or quarter but will soon move on to tenths and hundredths.

'Bull's-eye' can also be used to introduce the idea of

limits of accuracy. Different levels of play can introduce greater accuracy. In the example given in this activity you could give five different targets:

- Target 1 between 90 and 110;
- Target 2 between 99 and 101;
- Target 3 between 99.5 and 100.5;
- Target 4 between 99.9 and 100.1;
- Target 5 between 99.99 and 100.01.
  Other levels could also be added.

It is also possible to play the game by division. Give the children a starting number and ask what number they must divide by to obtain the target number.

The game can also be played using the multiply or divide constant. Using the above example, the children should key in:

23 ⊠ ⊠ (then the guess number) ▤

After this, they need only key in their guess each time:

5 ▤ gives 115
4.5 ▤ gives 103.5

Remind them not to use the ⌐AC⌐ key or the constant will also be cleared.

10. Crossover

Age range
Ten upwards.

Group size
Pairs.

What you need
A calculator for each player.

What to do

Give one player a starting number to key into her calculator. The numbers are not secret, and players need to know what their opponent's number is as they go along. Players must take turns to add to or subtract from their number in such a way that they do not cross over their opponent's current number. The player with the largest number subtracts, while the player with the lowest number adds.

Example game

Player A has a starting number of 12; Player B starts on 35.

- Player A: 12 + 7 = 19
- Player B: 35 − 3 = 32
- Player A: 19 + 10 = 29
- Player B: 32 − 2 = 30
- Player A: 29 + 0.5 = 29.5
- Player B: 30 − 0.1 = 29.9
- Player A: 29.5 + 0.25 = 29.75
- Player B: 29.9 − 0.14 = 29.76

And so on . . .

Children need to keep a record of their play which also provides a useful check and a diagnostic aid to their understanding of decimal fractions and of the decreasing significance of numbers after the decimal point.

6. Estimation and trial and improvement

Many children undertake mathematical computations, with or without a calculator, through a kind of blind faith. They assume that the answer must be right. They seldom check to ensure that they have not omitted a decimal point, or forgotten a zero, or to see if the answer makes sense in the context of the problem. Children must be encouraged to check their calculations, however they have been working.

However, children's ability to work mentally without pencil and paper or a calculator can be improved if estimation is highlighted as an important everyday skill. We all make mathematical estimates every day. Some are simple, based on experience, and may not use numbers at all; others use rounded numbers to provide a starting point for further calculations.

The calculator is useful in developing estimation skills, particularly when applied to more complex calculations of multiplication and division. Many of the traditional algorithms for these processes relied heavily on rules which were seldom understood, for example, counting back the decimal places in multiplication sums. A good understanding here will make children less calculator-dependent, and able to undertake complex calculations without any aids, should the need arise.

Guessing used to be prohibited in mathematics, but much has changed. Children are now encouraged to have a go at a problem, even though they may not be sure what might happen. But guesses need to be based on an estimate of what a likely or sensible answer will be. The skills of estimation therefore need to be developed at all stages of a child's mathematical education.

First guesses may not be accurate enough, and it is important for children to refine them, modifying the original information to make a new and more accurate estimate. This is the process of trial and improvement.

The activities in this chapter can be used to develop children's estimation skills in a number of computational areas, and to develop the skills needed in using trial and improvement methods.

1. Rounding numbers

Age range
Nine upwards.

Group size
Individuals or pairs.

What you need
Prepared sets of numbers, pencils, calculators.

What to do
This activity involves asking the children to round numbers to the nearest 10, 100 or 1000. Prepare some sets of numbers like those shown in the examples overleaf.

The children should round each number up or down, write them down and add the rounded answers with the calculator. Finally, they should compare their answer with the check answer.

You may at first need to discuss with the children the rules for rounding numbers. These are:
- 21, 22, 23 and 24 round down to 20;
- 25, 26, 27, 28 and 29 round up to 30.

Example 1
Round each of these numbers to the nearest 10 and add them up.
- 39
- 21
- 18
- 42
- 37

Check answer: 160

Example 2
Round these numbers to the nearest 100 and add them up:
- 3682
- 4215
- 3998
- 4150
- 973

Check answer: 17100

Example 3
Decimal numbers can be rounded to one, two or three decimal places. Round these numbers to two decimal places and add them up:
- 14.576
- 23.365
- 12.666
- 7.998

Check answer: 58.62.

Follow-up
Similar numbers and rounding activities can include work in metric measures:
- rounding centimetres to the nearest metre;
- rounding grams to the nearest kilogram;
- rounding millilitres to the nearest litre.

These activities can be used to reinforce work already done on rounding numbers. As the children grow more confident, ask them to work out the check answer for themselves.

2. In between

Age range
Ten upwards.

Group size

Pairs.

What you need

A calculator between two, a pack of prepared number cards, scoreboard.

What to do

Before beginning any computation, whether or not children are using a calculator, they should make an estimate of their answers to check them against reality. This game helps children to practise the estimation skills needed in division. This is particularly important when working with decimal fractions. Give each pair of children a pack of prepared cards with one number on each, a scoreboard and a calculator. Example scoreboards and playing numbers are shown below.

Scoreboard	
Answer	Scores
Between 0 and 1	1 point
Between 1 and 10	2 points
Between 10 and 100	3 points
Over 100	0 points

Playing numbers			
9	23	31	46
97	129	152	216
255	364	440	800
1974	2132	2561	1619
2815	3966	4770	9342
13000	14500	16000	29500

Ask them to spread out the number cards, face upwards. Each player should take turns to choose two number cards. Numbers may only be used once in each game.

Using a calculator, the child should divide the larger number by the smaller one and check the whole-number part of the answer against the scoreboard. The first player to reach ten points is the winner.

Follow-up

Alter the playing numbers to include numbers less than 1. This will provide useful reinforcement when introducing multiplication and division of decimals by decimals. Allow the players to use both multiplication and division in the same game. The scoreboard and playing numbers will need changing. For example:

Scoreboard	
Answer	Scores
Between 0 and 1	1 point
Between 0.1 and 0.0	2 points
Between 0.01 and 0.1	3 points
Over 1	0 points

Playing numbers			
0.9	2.3	3.1	4.6
0.8	1.25	1.32	2.06
0.2	0.4	0.3	0.8
0.04	0.12	0.34	0.28
0.36	0.39	0.58	0.54
0.47	3.56	3.56	9.86

3. First estimates for multiplication

Age range
Nine upwards.

Group size
Individuals or pairs.

What you need
One calculator between two, prepared worksheets, pencils.

What to do
Children need to develop strategies for estimating whether answers are correct. This activity will help them to check that multiplication answers are in the right order of accuracy: 100 not 10; 300 not 3000.

Give the children a prepared sheet with calculations similar to the ones below. Ask them to select two numbers from the ones given which will multiply together to give an answer closest to the one they need. They should not worry unduly about the effect of the units digits. Previous work on rounding numbers will be useful for this activity. However, the children will need to take into account whether they have rounded up or down. There could be more than one combination for some answers. When they have chosen their numbers, they may check the answer with their calculator. For example:

Choice numbers											
16	19	23	26	28	33	35	41	49	54		
1) _____23_____	×	_____28_____	=	650
2) _____	×	_____	=	300
3) _____	×	_____	=	1300
4) _____	×	_____	=	600
5) _____	×	_____	=	850
6) _____	×	_____	=	2200

4. More accurate estimation

Age range
Nine upwards.

Group size
Individuals or pairs.

What you need
One calculator between two, prepared worksheets, pencils.

What to do
This activity will help children to check multiplication answers using the multiplication of the two units digits to refine their first estimates based on rounding. For example, if the answer required ends in 8, children must select two numbers whose units digits make 8 when multiplied together.

Give the children prepared sheets with calculations similar to the ones below, and ask them to select which two numbers from the ones given will multiply together to give the correct answer. When they have chosen they may check the answer with their calculator.

```
                    Choice numbers
              11   12   16   23   31   39
1) _____16_____ × _____23_____ = 368
2) _____ × _____ = 192
3) _____ × _____ = 341
4) _____ × _____ = 372
5) _____ × _____ = 253
6) _____ × _____ = 496
```

5. Lines of four

Age range
Nine upwards.

Group size
Pairs or groups of three.

What you need
Calculators, two different coloured sets of counters, photocopiable pages 118 and 119.

What to do
This game can be played at many levels depending on the age and ability of the children. It will help to reinforce and develop estimation of multiplication and division.

Ask each player to choose a set of coloured counters. Give the players a copy of the grid on page 118. They must use only the numbers in the top box to make the numbers which appear in the playing grid.

If they are correct in selecting the two numbers which make their target number, they can cover that square with their own coloured counter. The aim of the game is to make a line of four counters of the same colour in any direction (vertical, horizontal or diagonal). The children can use the calculator to try out numbers and to check answers.

The use of the calculator can vary according to the concepts involved and the ability of the children. If children are playing in threes, only the third person should use the calculator to check each player's estimate. If a player is wrong, play passes to the opponent.

By using the blank photocopiable sheet on page 119, you can use your own numbers to help reinforce long multiplication estimation with large numbers. For example:

| 17 | 19 | 21 | 33 | 37 | 45 | 54 | 62 | 80 | × | = |

1665	2640	1360	1178	1782	1221
765	1680	2294	855	945	1302
1485	399	2790	777	3600	2430
1998	627	703	1302	1134	2960
1782	1454	561	629	1026	693
357	918	3348	2025	323	2046

Follow-up

Use the blank grid for work with equivalent decimal fractions, or for multiplication and division by decimal fractions.

A grid can also be made with hexagons, where the aim is to make a line joining one side of the board with the other.

To make the game more challenging, include some 'rogue' numbers in the grid. It should be impossible to make them from the given numbers.

6. Decimal multiplication

Age range
Ten upwards.

Group size
Individuals or pairs.

What you need
One calculator between two.

What to do

Give the children a sheet of prepared multiplications involving numbers with decimal fractions. Each number should appear twice, once as a whole number and then divided by 10 (57 and 5.7).

Ask the children to work out each pair of multiplication sums using a calculator.

Example

$67 \times 3 =$ _____	$6.7 \times 3 =$ _____
$145 \times 5 =$ _____	$14.5 \times 5 =$ _____
$22 \times 11 =$ _____	$2.2 \times 11 =$ _____
$17 \times 26 =$ _____	$17 \times 2.6 =$ _____
$45 \times 19 =$ _____	$45 \times 1.9 =$ _____
$83 \times 12 =$ _____	$83 \times 1.2 =$ _____
$59 \times 21 =$ _____	$5.9 \times 2.1 =$ _____

When the children have completed the examples, ask them to compare the two sets of answers. What do they notice about the digits in their answers?

Ask them to look at the answers to the questions in the

second box. Can they find a way of predicting the position of the decimal point in answers to calculations like these?

Follow-up

Similar examples can also be used to explore division involving numbers with decimal fractions. The effect of multiplying the two numbers by a factor of ten to remove the decimal point from the denominator is an interesting one to explore:

- 14202 $\div$ 18 $\boxed{=}$ _____
- 1420.2 $\div$ 1.8 $\boxed{=}$ _____
- 142.02 $\div$ 0.18 $\boxed{=}$ _____

Ask the childen to compile their own division sums that will all give the same answer.

7. Rounding and multiplying

Age range
Ten upwards.

Group size
Individuals or pairs.

What you need
A calculator between two, photocopiable page 120, pencils.

What to do
Give the children a photocopy of page 120. Ask them to make estimates of the answers to each question by

rounding the decimals to whole numbers. Although we have already discussed the usual rules for rounding (see page 59), for this activity, children should follow a different rule in each column, as shown on the photocopiable page.

When they have filled in the table, ask the children to check with the calculator and ring the best estimate. From their results, can they say which methods of estimating seem to give the best results for multiplication sums?

Follow-up
The same idea can be used to explore division involving numbers with decimal fractions.

8. Estimate and multiply

Age range
Ten upwards.

Group size
Individuals or pairs.

What you need
One calculator between two, photocopiable page 121, pencils.

What to do
Give each pair a photocopy of page 121. Ask the children to make a rough mental estimate of each sum and write it in the space provided.

In the same space, ask them to write how they made their estimate, and whether they think it might be too small, too big, or close.

Before checking the answer on the calculator, ask them to ring what they think is the right answer from those given.

Follow-up
Use the same format to explore division involving numbers with decimal fractions.

QUESTION	ESTIMATED ANSWER	POSSIBLE ANSWERS	CALCULATOR CHECK
3·82×2·27	4×2=8	4·0324 0·4024 8·6714 86·714	8·6714

9. How close can you get?

Age range
Nine upwards.

Group size
Individuals or pairs.

What you need
One calculator between two, prepared worksheets, pencils.

What to do
This activity can be used in many different forms:
● as a diagnostic tool for children's understanding of place value;
● to help develop estimation skills;
● to provide starting points for investigational work;
● to develop trial and improvement methods.

Give the children a copy of a prepared sheet of examples. For each problem, they must use each of the digits provided once only to make the target number, or where indicated, get as close to it as possible.

Example 1
In each case, use the digits 1, 2, 3, 4:
    [   ] × [   ] [   ] [   ]
    Make the biggest possible answer.
    [   ] [   ] × [   ] [   ]
    The answer is 448.
    [   ] [   ] [   ] ÷ [   ]
    The smallest possible answer.

10. Consecutive numbers

Age range
Nine upwards.

Group size
Individuals or pairs.

What you need
Calculators, pencils, paper.

What to do
Consecutive numbers are those which follow each other, such as 2, 3 and 4.

To begin with, ask the children which two consecutive numbers multiply together to make 12. Try some more examples with familiar numbers from tables work.

Then extend this to a larger number. Try 342. Allow children to use a calculator to try out some numbers. Make sure that they write down the numbers they try and the results so that they know which numbers they have used. Ask them to say whether their estimate is too big or too small in each case.

Discuss with them how they know what numbers to try next. This is the basis of all trial and improvement work. They should use the previous results to decide on the next numbers to use.

Follow-up
Once children have grasped this principle, they will be ready to try more complex problems. They can begin by trying three consecutive numbers and moving on to four. This will also allow them to practise their estimation skills.

Example 2
Use the digits provided to get as close as possible to the target number.

[   ] [   ] × [   ]
Digits 2 3 5, target 80.
[   ] [   ] × [   ] [   ]
Digits 1 2 3 4, target 500.

It is essential that children record their work in this activity, particularly for those problems where the target is the largest, or closest number. Some of the combinations give similar answers and careful recording is necessary to pick out the right combinations, and to encourage discussion on the strategies used.

11. What's the area?

Age range
Nine upwards.

Group size
Individuals or pairs.

What you need
One calculator between two, rectangle shapes with different areas, paper, pencils.

What to do

Given a rectangle, children are usually asked to work out its area by using its length and breadth. However, this activity is just the opposite. Children must try to work out the possible dimensions of the rectangle, starting from the area. The children will have to think of some starting numbers and then gradually refine their estimates to get closer to the area.

Once again it is important that children record the results as they work, otherwise they will forget which numbers they have tried. As in the 'Bull's-eye' activity (see page 56), you may want to set some limits to the required accuracy.

Example
Area of rectangle: 31cm^2.
● Try 1: $10 \times 3 = 30$ (too small).
● Try 2: $11 \times 3 = 33$ (too big).
● Try 3: $10.5 \times 3 = 31.5$ (too big).
You might give younger children one of the dimensions and ask them to work out the other one.

Follow-up

The same process can be used with older pupils to find the dimensions of a cube with a given volume. Obviously, in this instance the children must work with three different dimensions.

Example
Volume of cube $= 46 \text{cm}^3$.
● Try 1: $4 \times 3 \times 4 = 48 \text{cm}^3$.
● Try 2: $4 \times 3 \times 3.5 = 42 \text{cm}^3$.
● Try 3: $4 \times 3 \times 3.8 = 45.6 \text{cm}^3$.
This is certainly a more difficult task than working on areas!

12. Square roots and products

Age range
Ten upwards.

Group size
Individuals or pairs.

What you need
A calculator between two, paper, pencils.

What to do
Ask the children to solve some of the following problems using only trial and improvement methods. They may use a calculator if they wish and should keep a record of their work.

Square roots
Although the calculator has a square root key, it is often interesting to ask children to work out square roots by trial and improvement.

Select a number and ask children to find the square root (the powers key is useful in this work). For example, to find the square root of 12, key:
- 3.5 ☒ ☰ 12.25.
- 3.4 ☒ ☰ 11.56.

You can keep on trying with closer and closer approximations, but this method cuts down on the keying and the possibility of mistakes when the numbers become longer.

For the keen investigator, cube roots add another dimension to the calculations. A similar keying process can be used. To find the cube root of 70, for all calculations, key:

- 4 ☒ ☒ ☰ ☰ 64.
- 4.5 ☒ ☒ ☰ ☰ 91.125 . . .

Products and sums
If the sum of two numbers is 10 and their product is 21, what are they?

Discuss with the children strategies for solving this so that they can be shared by a wider number of children. Some children may have started by choosing numbers at random and seeing what happened when they added and multiplied them together. Others might have started by finding two numbers which when added made 10 and seeing if they came to 21 when multiplied together. Still others will start from the multiplication part.

Follow-up
It will not be long before the more able, or enterprising, discover that they can short-circuit some of the trial and improvement problems by working backwards using division. Although this means you will have to insist on them following the original process, it does highlight the fact that the child has grasped the important mathematical concept that multiplication is the reverse operation to division. Ask such children to make up some problems for other children to solve where division cannot be used to solve the problem.

7. Number patterns and investigations

It is vital that investigatory work and the use of the calculator become an integral part of the mathematics curriculum, and are not regarded as extra activities that are sometimes indulged in.

Investigatory work provides opportunities for skills to be practised in unfamiliar situations. Using a calculator adds another dimension. It helps to develop children's understanding of number and can develop a child's interest in and fascination with number patterns. Investigational work involves the following processes:

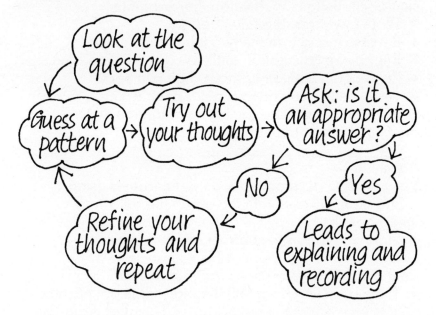

The calculator provides support for this approach. The computational powers of the calculator allow many examples to be tried while children look for a pattern or rule. This means they do not need to spend large amounts of time on routine calculations; the children can concentrate on the problem in hand. This becomes a motivating factor.

Investigations give children the opportunity to work in pairs or small groups, to talk and to question each other's ideas. This is a vital stage in the process and should not be hurried. Explaining verbally to others often leads to greater understanding. Using the calculator gives children confidence in the accuracy of their calculations. The stages of reasoning will need to be recorded in a variety of ways, creating a more flexible approach.

You may feel reluctant to embark on this kind of work, because an investigation will often have no single or clear-cut answer. However, this and the wide range of trials a calculator makes possible should be seen as an advantage and a challenge.

This chapter gives some ideas for starting number investigations. Establishing an open-ended approach, where teacher and children can question and develop their thoughts together, is essential if these activities are to become interesting, meaningful and exciting. From these starting points, further work can be developed, and the children may find their own interesting lines of enquiry.

1. Palindromic numbers

Age range
Nine to eleven.

Group size
Pairs or small groups.

What you need
Calculators, pencils, paper.

What to do

A palindromic number reads the same backwards as forwards; for example, these numbers are all palindromes: 171; 515; 666; 797; 69096.

Discuss with the children the word 'palindromic'. Ask the class to find out what it means before dividing up to work on activities appropriate to their ability.

Activity 1

Ask the children to use the constant function to set their calculator to 'add 1'. Now let them try to solve the following questions.
- Which numbers between 10 and 50 are palindromes?
- Which numbers between 50 and 100 are palindromes?
- Which is the largest palindrome under 100?
- Which numbers between 100 and 200 are palindromes?
- Which is the largest palindrome under 500?
- Which is the smallest palindrome over 500?
- List the palindromes between 200 and 1000.

After the initial discussion, it might be useful to prepare similar ideas on a worksheet for the groups to examine.

Activity 2

Many, but not all numbers, can be made into palindromes by reversing and then adding together. For example:
- 246
- Reversed: 642
- Added together: 642
  246

  888

If it doesn't work at first, it will probably work after a few reversals:
- Start number: 362
- Reversed: 263
- Added together: 625
- Reversed: 526
- Added together: 1151
- Reversed: 1511
- Added together: 2662.

Discuss this activity with the children. Give them similar challenges to develop. For example:
- Write any three-digit number.
- Reverse it and add the two numbers together.
- Repeat the calculation until you get a palindrome.
- Try it again with other three-digit numbers.
- Test whether you always get a palindrome.
- It is also possible to try this investigation with two-digit numbers. What happens?

Activity 3

You can also develop work on palindromes using subtraction. Discuss with the group the following investigations.
- Start with 888, and subtract any two-digit palindrome. What happens? Is your answer a palindrome? Give reasons for your answer.
- Try subtracting from 888 the three-digit palindrome 262. Is your answer a palindrome? Try other three-digit palindromes. Will you always end with a palindrome? Why?

Activity 4

Introduce the multiplication of palindromes to the children. Which palindromes between 10 and 100 can be multiplied by themselves to give another palindrome?

Activity 5

Some numbers are palindromic and are also divisible by 7, for instance 77 and 161. Let the children use the constant function to set up $\boxplus$ 7. Ask them to make a list of the numbers that are divisible by 7. Are there any more palindromes between 100 and 999 which are divisible by 7? Can they find a rule?

Encourage them to write down all palindromes between 1000 and 9999 which are divisible by 7. Can they still use their rule? Let them discuss their findings and record them for someone else to follow.

Using these examples, encourage the groups to discuss their findings and to question each other's reasoning. This will help them to clarify their view and strengthen their understanding.

2. Fibonacci sequence

Age range
Ten to twelve.

Group size
Six to eight children.

What you need
Calculators, pencils, paper.

What to do
Introduce the children to the work of a famous Italian mathematician, Leonardo Fibonacci (1170–1230). The Fibonacci Sequence of number, which he spotted and investigated, starts as follows:
1 1 2 3 5 8 13 21 34 55 89 144 . . .

Many investigations have been linked with this series of numbers and a few starting points are given below. It is worth while to develop work on this in two ways. You can look at the work of Fibonacci in its own right. Many history books contain accounts of this great man's life and work. Equally interesting is the investigation into the patterns he developed.

Investigation 1
Starting with 2, each number is the sum of the previous two numbers. Let the children use a calculator to calculate the next ten numbers in the sequence.

Investigation 2
Ask the children to use the Fibonacci Sequence to investigate the following:
- The sum of the first three numbers is one less than the 5th.
- The sum of the first four numbers is one less than the 6th.
- The sum of the first five numbers is one less than the 7th.
- Can the pattern be continued?
- What do you notice?

Investigation 3
There are many interesting patterns which can be developed from the series. Ask the children to choose a number in the series, for example, 89. Ask them to find the product of the numbers on either side of the chosen number. In this case, $55 \times 144 = 7920$. Let them square the number they first chose. $89^2 = 7921$.

The difference between the product of the numbers either side of the chosen number and the square of the number should be 1. Is this always so? Encourage the children to try other numbers.

3. Happy numbers

Age range
Eight to twelve.

Group size
Pairs or small groups.

What you need
Calculators, pencils, paper.

What to do
A number is 'happy' if, when you square the digits in this number and add and repeat this process, you eventually arrive at 1. For example, try 31:
$3^2 + 1^2 = 9 + 1 = 10$.
$1^2 + 0^2 = 1$.
Try 13: $1^2 + 3^2 = 1 + 9 = 10$. $1^2 + 0^2 = 1 + 0 = 1$.
It follows that 31 and 13 are happy numbers. You could set the following problems:
- Can the children show that 11 is a happy number?
- Is 12 happy?
- Is 29 happy?
- How many happy numbers lie between 1 and 99?
 Once the groups have tried some of these lines of investigation, invite them to generate their own questions to ask others.

4. Number chains

Age range
Eight to twelve.

Group size
Pairs or small groups.

What you need
Calculators, pencils, prepared worksheets, photocopiable pages 122, 123 and 124.

What to do
Activity 1
Look at the flow chart given below. Discuss the activity with the groups, and then prepare appropriate examples for them on a worksheet.

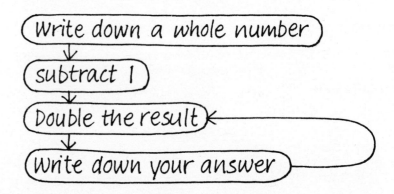

 Encourage them to keep writing down the series of numbers. Ask them questions such as:
- Can you spot any patterns developing in the series of numbers you generate?
- Can you explain what you have found?

74

Let them work through the same number chain sequence using other start numbers. Can they see a pattern developing now?

Activity 2
Let the children use different starting numbers with these chains and see what happens.

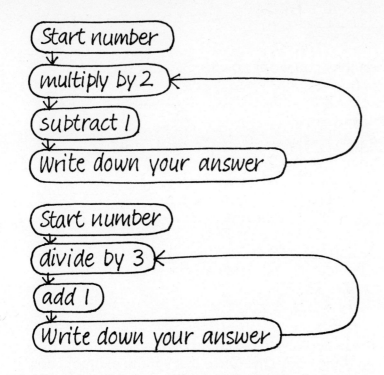

Discuss their findings with the children and encourage them to look for more than one relationship. Can they develop their own number chains?

Activity 3
Number chains can be written down in a variety of ways. Here are further examples of this type of investigation.

Using different starting numbers, ask the children to see what results are produced by the following chains: What do they notice about the results?

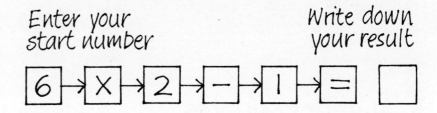

Activity 4
Let the children try a mystery number chain:

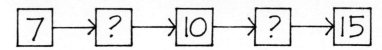

Can they find the numbers which are added on at each stage? A more complicated chain can also be developed.

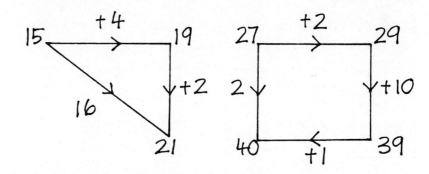

Compile a worksheet containing examples, starting with the simplest chains.

Follow-up

Having tried the various ways of recording, use the number chains on photocopiable pages 122, 123 and 124 to give more examples. The blank sheets may also encourage the children to develop their own chains.

5. Number squares

Age range

Seven to eleven.

Group size

Six to ten children.

What you need

Calculators, squared paper, pencils, a prepared worksheet.

What to do

Draw out an example of a multiplication number square like the one shown below.

6	4	
7	2	

Ask the children to look at the number square and fill in the spaces by multiplying the numbers together.

Initially, they should work across.

$6 \times 4 = 24$
$7 \times 2 = 14$

6	4	24
7	2	14

Then they can work down.

$6 \times 7 = 42$
$4 \times 2 = 8$

6	4	24
7	2	14
42	8	336

For the last number let them check:
$42 \times 8 = 336$
$24 \times 14 = 336$

These two answers should be the same if the work has been done correctly. Once this simple example has been discussed, give the children a worksheet with further examples. Invite the children to devise their own problems for others to investigate.

6. Consecutive numbers

Age range
Eight to eleven.

Group size
Six to ten children.

What you need
Calculators, pencils, squared paper.

What to do
Ensure that the children understand the term 'consecutive numbers'. Then discuss the following investigations.

Investigation 1
- $14 + 15 = 29$
- $[\quad] + [\quad] = 13$
- $[\quad] + [\quad] = 17$
- $[\quad] + [\quad] = 25$

Can the children work out how to find the consecutive numbers that add up to the totals given? Is there a rule that always works?

Investigation 2
Ask the children for three consecutive numbers. Let them multiply the first by the last and write down their answer. They should then square the middle number and write it down. Can they find the difference between their two answers? For example:
- $12, 13, 14$
- $12 \times 14 = 168$

- $13^2 = 169$
- $169 - 168 = 1$

Let them repeat the activity using other consecutive strings. Can they spot a pattern? Ask them to try other number sequences. What happens?

Investigation 3
Investigate with the children the multiplication of consecutive numbers. Can they find two consecutive numbers that, when multiplied together, produce the totals given?
- $10 \times 11 = 110$
- $[\quad] \times [\quad] = 210$
- $[\quad] \times [\quad] = 650$
- $[\quad] \times [\quad] = 182$
- $[\quad] \times [\quad] = 342$
- $[\quad] \times [\quad] = 2756$

Investigation 4
Let the children multiply two consecutive numbers together. Can they discover which number these answers are always exactly divisible by?
- $6 \times 7 =$
- $7 \times 8 =$
- $17 \times 18 =$
- $23 \times 24 =$

Ask them to do the same with three consecutive numbers.
- $2 \times 3 \times 4 =$
- $5 \times 6 \times 7 =$
- $8 \times 9 \times 10 =$

Which number are these answers divisible by?
Now let them try it with four consecutive numbers.

7. Number investigation

Age range
Eight to eleven.

Group size
Pairs or small groups.

What you need
Calculators, pencils, paper.

What to do
Discuss with the children the following investigation and ask them to carry out the instructions.

- Write a three digit number: 123

- Reverse it: 321

- Subtract the smaller number:

$$\begin{array}{r} 321 \\ -\ 123 \\ \hline 198 \end{array}$$

- Reverse your answer: 891

- Add the two numbers together: 1089

  Ask the children to try other examples using their calculators. This will speed the process and enable them to concentrate on searching for a rule. Do they always get 1089? Are other answers possible?

  There are three conclusions to this investigation.

- 0 is obtained when the number used is a palindrome:

$$\begin{array}{r} 212 \\ 212 \\ \hline 000 \end{array}$$

- 198 is obtained when the difference between the first and the last digit is 1:

$$\begin{array}{r} 213 \\ 312 \\ \hline 312 \\ -213 \\ \hline 99 \\ +\ 99 \\ \hline 198 \end{array}$$

- 1089 is obtained when the difference between the first and the last digit is 2 or more:

$$\begin{array}{r} 129 \\ 921 \\ \hline 921 \\ -129 \\ \hline 792 \\ +297 \\ \hline 1089 \end{array}$$

  Once the children have carried out various examples, encourage them to discuss their findings and to try to record them systematically to produce the above rules. Do not explain the rule before the children have investigated it for themselves.

$$213 \quad 312 - 213 = 99 + 99 = 198$$

8. Multiples of eleven

Age range
Eight to eleven.

Group size
Six to ten children.

What you need
Calculators, pencils, paper, a prepared worksheet.

What to do
Discuss with the children the following examples and let them use a calculator to work out the answers.

- 13 ⊠ 11 ⊟
- 14 ⊠ 11 ⊟
- 27 ⊠ 11 ⊟
- 45 ⊠ 11 ⊟
- 98 ⊠ 11 ⊟

Can they use their results to spot a way of working out the answer without using the calculator?

Prepare a worksheet of further examples similar to those shown below. Ask the children to work out the answers to the problems and then use a calculator to check their answer.

- 48 ⊠ 11 ⊟
- 72 ⊠ 11 ⊟
- 28 ⊠ 11 ⊟
- 69 ⊠ 11 ⊟
- 76 ⊠ 11 ⊟

The children should consider whether their method works for three-, four- and five-digit numbers. Ask them to use the calculator to try some examples, and then see whether the method works. Can they work out the following
problems without using a calculator?

- 157 ⊠ 11 ⊟
- 386 ⊠ 11 ⊟
- 1638 ⊠ 11 ⊟
- 9825 ⊠ 11 ⊟

8. Memory, percentages and negative numbers

This chapter covers three important uses of the calculator which can enhance mathematical work at a more advanced level. First, we look at the memory keys, and detailed examples are given that will enable children to understand the value of using them. Secondly, the percentage key is explained. Its potential is shown with examples from VAT calculations and discounts on sale goods. Finally, we see how the calculator can be an invaluable tool in illustrating the world of negative numbers.

1. Memory chains

Age range
Nine to eleven.

Group size
Six to eight children.

What you need
Identical simple calculators, pencils, paper.

What to do
The memory keys are probably the least used keys on the simple calculator. They allow parts of a calculation to be stored and retrieved. As explained in Chapter 1, the keys usually found on a simple calculator are:
- M+ memory plus;
- M− memory minus;
- MR memory recall.

To use the memory facility, a chain or sequence of key presses has to be employed. Having examined your calculator's memory keys, discuss with the group the sequence for the following calculation:
46 − (12 + 4)
Using the memory, the following keys have to be pressed:
- 46 is put into the display;
- M+ puts 46 into the memory;
- C clears the display (this is not vital but helps to show the different parts of the calculation to the children);
- 12 ⊞ 4 works out the part in brackets;
- M− subtracts the bracketed calculation from the number stored in the memory;
- MR gives you what is now in the memory – the answer to the whole calculation;
- AC clears the memory.

Give the group various examples to work through, asking them to record their key presses as they go.

Follow-up
Encourage the children to develop the chains for the following calculations:
- 22 − (10 + 5);
- 245 − (84 + 77);
- 78 − (14 + 45);
- 154 + (89 − 45).

Would the chain for a calculation like (17 + 69) − (19 + 4) be different? If so, how and why?

Use other calculations to suit the class's ability. The children can work in pairs to predict the sequence and to test their thoughts.

2. Careful planning

Age range
Eleven upwards.

Group size
Six to eight children.

What you need
Simple calculators, paper, pencils.

What to do
Using the memory makes complex calculations easier to solve. You can only store one number at a time, so planning the order of calculations is important. In division or subtraction, it is important to work out the second part of the sum first and to store the answer in the memory so that you are dividing into or subtracting from the correct part of the sum. You will need to explain this carefully to the group. One of the easiest ways of tackling this is to work with the children through examples like this:

$$\frac{26 + 39}{21 + 6}$$

The chain of key presses would be:
- 21 $\boxplus$ 6
- $\boxed{M+}$
- $\boxed{C}$
- 26 $\boxplus$ 39
- $\boxed{\div}$
- $\boxed{MR}$
- $\boxed{=}$
- 2.4074074

Again, it is important to encourage the group to talk through what is happening and why at every stage, to demonstrate a clear grasp of the process involved in using the memory keys.

Provide the children with further examples to let them practise the sequence for division and subtraction. Encourage them to estimate first to check that they are getting a reasonable answer.

Examples:
- $$\frac{38 - 15}{12 + 2}$$

- $$\frac{45 + 70}{85 - 21}$$

3. Memory prediction

Age range
Eleven upwards.

Group size
Pairs.

What you need
Simple calculators, prepared worksheets, pencils.

What to do
Give each pair a worksheet that has chains of key presses already determined. Use examples like the one shown below.
- 20 $\boxtimes$ 10 $\boxed{M+}$
- 5 $\boxtimes$ 10 $\boxed{M-}$
- 7 $\boxtimes$ 10 $\boxed{M-}$

- 6 ⊠ 10 M−
- Predict what the memory holds.
- MR
- AC

Follow-up
Once the children have worked out the strategy being used, you could set up the activity as a memory challenge for each pair. One child could set the problem while the other predicts the answer. They can then check using the calculator.

4. Memory store

Age range
Eleven upwards.

Group size
Six to eight children.

What you need
Simple calculators, paper, pencils.

What to do
Explain to the children that there is another use for the calculator's memory. It can be used to store a number to save entering it over and over again. If you are working out, say, a money problem which calls for many subtractions from one pound (100 pence), the following chain could be used instead of entering 100 every time.
100 M+ C MR − 32 = 68
MR will bring the 100 back and you can continue.

Explain each stage before demonstrating the next, making sure the children understand. Ask them to follow the instructions until they are familiar with this procedure. Then challenge them to use this memory method to develop other number problems.

5. Speed and efficiency challenge

Age range
Eleven upwards.

Group size
Six to eight children.

What you need
Calculators, pencil, paper.

What to do
Explain to the group that using the memory helps them to become more proficient and reduces the time they take to carry out a calculation. They have no need to write down a subtotal part way through a calculation. Use the following example to demonstrate:
(2.00×16) + (5.50×8)
To work out this question you do the first multiplication and store the answer in the memory:
£2.00 ⊠ 16 M+
Then the second multiplication has to be done:
£5.50 ⊠ 8 M+
The memory now holds the combined totals for both calculations. To display the total the children must press MR .

Follow-up

Group the children into pairs and give them a worksheet containing examples like the one shown above. Ask one child to carry out the work using a calculator but without using the memory keys, and let the second child use the memory facilities. Ask them which method is more efficient, and which method requires written support and why.

6. Memory investigation

Age range

Ten to twelve.

Group size

Individuals or groups.

What you need

Worksheets, calculators, pencils.

What to do

Setting a practical situation that involves using the calculator's memory is important. It enables the children to transfer their present skills and to develop them in a relevant context. You may be planning a school visit where costs have to be calculated, or you may be selling books in a school bookshop where accounts have to be kept. If you can obtain real data for the children to use, it becomes more meaningful. If, however, this is not possible, you could use a mathematical investigation similar to the one given here to set the context.

A school trip to a theme park is being planned. The children have to pay different prices for different rides. The rides have to be paid for in advance by the school.
The price list gives the following information:
- The roller coaster costs £1.00.
- The white water run costs £0.50.
- The big wheel costs £0.50.
- The ghost train costs £0.75.
- The pirate ship costs £0.60.
- The train ride costs £1.25.

A survey of the children reveals that:
- 46 want to go on the roller coaster;
- 39 want to go on the white water;
- 81 want to go on the big wheel;
- 20 want to go on the ghost train;
- 53 want to go on the pirate ship;
- 41 want to go on the train ride.

Ask the children to write down the key sequences, using the memory keys to help. What will be the total cost of the rides?

Recording and discussion are important and should be encouraged.

The supermarket could provide another source of memory calculations, especially keeping a check on what you spend as you go around:

- 3 loaves at 67p   3 ⊠ 0.67 ⊟ M+ ;
- 4 tins of beans at 24p   4 ⊠ 0.24 ⊟ M+.

Then MR brings up the total.

7. Percentage key

Age range
Eight to twelve.

Group size
Any.

What you need
Calculators, pencils, paper.

What to do
Discuss with the group the position of the % key on the calculator. This key should only be used when the children have previously worked on percentages and understand the concept.

As the calculator cannot handle fractions in the conventional way, a decimal approach is important. If you are going to use the calculator for percentage work, it is vital that the children have practised converting fractions to decimal fractions. Use the calculator to divide the top by the bottom. This should involve improper as well as proper fractions. For example

- $\dfrac{75}{100} = 0.75$

- $\dfrac{132}{76} = 1.73$

To find the answer to 25 per cent of 70 using the % key, the children must enter the number 70, then multiply by the percentage they want and press the % key. The chain of key presses is:

- 70
- ⊠
- 25
- %

The calculator actually performs the sum 70×0.25 which gives 17.5. If there is no % key, the child needs to understand the link between percentages and decimal fractions and key in 70 ⊠ 0.25 or 0.25 ⊠ 70.

Discuss this activity with the group. Give them more examples and ask them to record the calculation and the answers. Can they work out the sums without using the % key? Can they record this method?

8. VAT attack

Age range
Ten to twelve.

Group size
Six to eight children.

What you need
Simple calculators, pencils, paper.

What to do
Use the concept of Value Added Tax to give children a real situation for using the ☒% key on a simple calculator. The current rate of VAT is 17.5%. Most goods bought in shops have VAT already added. However, in some warehouses, builders' merchants and so on, the price of items excludes VAT. Make a collection of catalogues, price lists and mailing leaflets for such items. Discuss with the group how the calculator could be used to work out the prices plus VAT, in other words, the selling prices. It is important for the children to talk through the key presses they will need to make and record them; the order of key presses is crucial. Giving an example to focus on may prove helpful to the children's understanding and help you to identify their train of thought.

Example
- A new bath costs £195 excluding VAT. What is the actual selling price?
- VAT is 17.5% of £195.
- VAT: 195 ☒ 17.5 % is 34.125 rounded to £34.13
- Selling price: 195 ⊞ 34.13 ⊟ £229.13

Give them some other examples too. Encourage the children to work on investigating costs with and without VAT for complete room layouts, perhaps for a bathroom or kitchen.

As the children progress, they can be introduced to the shorter method of working out the sale price including VAT:
£195 ☒ 17.5 % ⊞ gives £229.125.

9. Discounts

Age range
Ten to twelve.

Group size
Six to eight children.

What you need
Simple calculators, paper, pencils.

What to do
The % key is also useful for working out discounts. We often see signs offering percentage reductions on original selling prices. Discuss with the children discounts they have seen or heard about. Ask them, 'How could the % key be used to solve a discount question?' Give them an example like the one here to focus the discussion.

Example
15% reduction is offered for cash on a new mountain bike, priced £130. What would the discount be? What would you have to pay?

Ask the children to predict and record the key presses they think will be needed. They should then check their predictions using the calculator.

- Discount is 15% of £130
- 130 ⊠ 15 %
- Discount = £19.50
- Price to pay is 130 ⊟ 19.50 ⊟ £110.50

As the children become more proficient with the use of the % key, they can link this activity with the memory key:

130 ⊠ 15 % M+ 130 ⊟ MR ⊟ £110.50.

You can also introduce a shorter method once the children are used to the memory key:

130 ⊠ 15 % ⊟ gives the answer in a single keying sequence.

10. Percentage investigations

Age range
Ten to twelve.

Group size
Any.

What you need
Calculators, pencils, paper.

What to do
Set the children some examples like those shown below. The aim is to encourage them to investigate the new and old prices of articles, and to try to find a connection between the percentage increase and the answer to the new price divided by the old price.

Investigation 1
After the budget, all prices went up by 12%. For each article, check the new price and divide it by the old price.

- A coat used to cost £24. New price: £26.88.

$$\frac{26.88}{24.00} =$$

- A pair of shoes used to cost £19.50. New price: £21.84.

$$\frac{21.84}{19.50} =$$

- A ball used to cost £5.00. New price: £5.60.

$$\frac{5.60}{5.00} =$$

Ask the children to look at the results gained by dividing the new price by the old, and try to find a connection with the percentage increase. They should discuss and record anything that they may notice.

Investigation 2
On a worksheet of similar examples, divide the new price by the old price. Study the answers and write down the percentage increase. For example:

- The old price was £6.20
- The new price is £8.00.
- $\dfrac{\text{New price}}{\text{Old price}} = \dfrac{£8.00}{£6.20}$
- What is the percentage increase?

Follow-up

Similar work could also be carried out using the idea of price reductions. For example, a coat offered in a sale shows the following price tickets. Ask the children to work out the percentage reduction in price.

- Old price: £40.00
- New price: £35.20
- $\dfrac{\text{New price}}{\text{Old price}} \quad \dfrac{35.20}{40.00} = 0.88$
- Percentage reduction = 100 − 88 =

11. Grandmother's gift

Age range

Eleven to twelve.

Group size

Any.

What you need

Photocopiable page 125, calculators, pencils, advertising literature from banks and building societies showing rates of interest.

What to do

Discuss with the children how savings in a bank earn interest. Show them some banks' advertising literature. Then set the following investigation for the children to tackle.

£1.00 earning interest at 8% grows year by year at the following rate:

Year 1   £1.00
Year 2   £1.08
Year 3   £1.17

Work out what the original 1.00 would have grown to in the fourth and fifth years.

Method 1

1.00 ⊠ 8 ⅍ ⊞ ⊟
1.08 ⊠ 8 ⅍ ⊞

Method 2

Set up constant, for example
1.08 ⊠ ⊠
Start at 1.00
⊟ ⊟ ⊟ generates the number sequences.

Give each child a photocopy of page 125 and ask them to work through the following question.

Suppose your great-grandmother had left £1.00 in a bank in 1901 to share among her heirs in 1999. Presume that it had been steadily growing at an interest rate of 8% (1.08).

Complete the table on the sheet showing how the money has grown and discuss the results.

12. Negative numbers

Age range
Seven to eleven.

Group size
Six to eight children.

What you need
Calculators, pencils, photocopiable page 126.

What to do
It is important to introduce the children to the idea of negative numbers in a very practical way before you introduce the calculator as a supportive tool. Children need to move from practical examples, such as a thermometer, to using a number line in conjunction with a calculator. Here the calculator offers an extra dimension to the usual work found in mathematics textbooks.

Before carrying out any examples, it is important to establish how negative numbers are displayed on the children's calculators. See Chapter 1 for clarification.

Let the children investigate the problems on the photocopiable sheet (see page 126). This should reinforce their understanding of how negative numbers are displayed.

13. Subtracting

Age range
Seven to eleven.

Group size
Six to ten children.

What you need
Calculators, pencils, paper.

What to do
Prepare a number line for each child, marked from −10 to +10. Explain to the group that a number line can be helpful in doing subtraction sums. For example, to find the answer to '7−4', you start at seven on the number line, move back four, and land on three, which is the answer.

Ask the children to do the following subtractions using their own number lines and then to check the answers on their calculators.

- 4−6
- 8−10
- 12−15
- 3−5
- 9−10
- 4−4
- 2−5
- 8−9

14. Negative and positive

Age range
Seven to eleven.

Group size
Any.

What you need
Calculators, pencils, paper.

What to do
Explain to the children that as subtraction sums move us back along a number line, addition sums move us forward. For example, to work out '4−6+3', we start at four on the line, move back six, and then move forward three, finishing on the number one.

Give the children some more questions like this. Encourage the groups to use the number line and then to check the answers with their calculators.

15. Negative match

Age range
Seven to eleven.

Group size
Any.

What you need
Calculators, pencils, paper.

What to do
Prepare a worksheet using examples similar to the ones shown below. Discuss with the children the need to use a calculator to help them link together the sums that have the same answer. Work through an example to help them clarify their thinking.

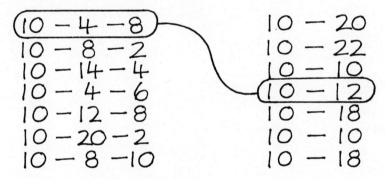

Ask the children to study their answers carefully, then supply sums to complete the links below.

$$10 - 4 - 10 \quad\longrightarrow\quad 10 - \square$$
$$10 - 12 - 4 \qquad\qquad 10 - \square$$
$$10 - 6 - 6 \qquad\qquad 10 - \square$$

9. Problem-solving

Although problem-solving has long been a part of primary school mathematics, its development has been patchy. Children often find it difficult to connect the kind of problems outlined in a traditional maths book with those they and their family encounter in the world outside school. This may be because, in real situations, there are no clues about the type of maths to use. We are not told to share or add, and the numbers encountered in actual situations are often more difficult to handle.

Recently, schools have begun to explore problems that children encounter in real life. These, rather than the often contrived examples found in mathematics schemes, have been used as starting points for mathematics. The concepts and skills involved draw upon the whole primary curriculum and put in a meaningful context the mathematics children use.

The activities suggested here encourage children to discuss and share ideas, plan, collect and collate information, look for relationships, make out a case, draw conclusions and take decisions.

Three clear processes can be identified when children work with everyday problem-solving:
- deciding what mathematics is necessary;
- carrying out the calculation;
- asking whether the answer makes sense.

The calculator is an invaluable aid to this process of problem-solving, but it does not answer questions for the children. It cannot think for itself. Children must still decide what sum to do, carry out the calculation and interpret the answer.

When children are deciding what mathematics is appropriate, the calculator can give them the confidence to make a start on a problem. They may decide to try a couple of specific cases which may then provide the impetus to move further into the problem.

When they have decided what type of mathematics is needed, the calculator again becomes an important tool. It allows children to focus their attention on the problem itself without having to worry about the computational aspects.

This chapter provides some ideas that can be adapted for use in your own teaching situation. Some actual examples are given but they are meant as starting points. Much more meaningful work will develop when the children use real data which they have collected themselves.

1. Feed the class

Age range
Nine to eleven.

Group size
Pairs or small groups.

What you need
Calculators, pencils, paper.

What to do
Planning a class party could be an interesting starting point for problem-solving. Ask the children to find out how much the party would cost to organise if a specific number of items were bought for each child. For example:
- Crisps 22p
- Sausage roll 25p

- Burger 30p
- Drink 21p

Using the prices above, how much would it cost to provide food for one child at the party? How much would it cost if all the class came?

Follow-up

Encourage the children to organise their recording, and give them opportunities to explain how they have gone about solving the problem. Supplementary questions could be given to confident children. For example, what would be the cost of organising a party for two classes in the school? What would be the cost for the whole school? Have the teachers been included in the costing?

2. Bonfire party

Age range

Ten to twelve.

Group size

Pairs or small groups.

What you need

Calculators, paper, pencils.

What to do

In this activity the calculator is used as an aid to solving real-life problems involving money. During the activity, encourage the children to discuss, plan and estimate costs as well as using the calculator.

The children should plan and record the cost of financing a bonfire party. This will allow them to demonstrate their calculator skills in a meaningful way. Discuss with them the approaches and functions which can be used to make the most effective use of the calculator.

Ask the children to plan the cost of the bonfire party under two headings, refreshments and entertainment. Refreshments should be calculated as costs per person and the children should construct an itemised list. Entertainment should include the fixed costs of fireworks, wood, rent of site, safety precautions and any other costs they can think of.

Example
- Food and drink per person:

Hot dog	£0.50
Cola	£0.30
Orange	£0.30
Crisps	£0.20
Baked potato	£0.40
Total per person	£1.70

- Entertainment (fixed costs):

Fireworks	£200.00
Site fees	£20.00
Wood	£30.00
First aid	£20.00
Total	£270.00

Suggest to the children that they make their own lists of items they feel are relevant and find out the correct costs of each item. Having carried out the initial research, the groups should discuss and plan how much the party would cost if the following numbers of people were invited. This information could be presented on a worksheet.

- 10 people
- 15 people
- 20 people
- 25 people
- 30 people
- 35 people
- 40 people

Ask the children to calculate the cost per person as well as the total cost. How would they reach their answers? They should record their method, and the functions they have used on the calculator.

There are many possible ways of recording. For example, when ten people are invited:

- Food per person: £1.70
- Cost of food for 10 people: £17.00
- Fixed cost: £270.00
- Total cost: £287.00
- Divided by 10: £28.70.

Once the group has developed a strategy for calculating the cost per person, ask them some other questions.

- If 100 people were invited, what would the cost be? How much would the school have to charge each individual if they wanted to make £50.00 profit to give to charity?
- If the school had limited funds, how many people could attend if they spent £450.00? How many could attend for £500.00, £550.00 or £600.00?

It is important to remind the children that the total cost is made up of the fixed cost and the variable cost. Will all the money be spent?

Follow-up

Develop similar problems using actual events that are taking place in school.

3. Electricity costs

Age range
Ten to twelve.

Group size
Pairs or small groups.

What you need
Calculators, pencils, paper, Electricity Board price lists.

What to do
Collect a price list of different tariff charges from your local Electricity Board. Discuss with the children the different rates shown. As an example, Economy 7 prices might be as follows:
- From 24.00 to 07.00hrs (night) each unit costs 2.60 pence.
- From 07.00 to 24.00hrs (day) each units cost 8.09 pence.

Explain to the children that you can work out the cost of using electrical appliances by looking at the wattage on them. One unit of electricity is 1 kilowatt or 1000 watts. Emphasise the safety factor at this point. Appliances should only be handled when unplugged from the mains.

Devise problems based on electricity charges for the children to solve. For example, an electric heater uses two kilowatts, which means two units per hour. At night, on Economy 7, it would cost 2×2.60 pence per hour (about 5 pence per hour to the nearest penny). What would the cost be if the heater was on during the day for one hour?

What would the following items cost per hour during the day?
- An electric immersion heater using 3 kilowatts.
- A microwave using 1.2 kilowatts.
- A cooker using 7.5 kilowatts.

Follow-up
- Ask the groups to list the electrical appliances they would like to find in a kitchen equipped for a family of four. They should find out the wattage of each item. Ask them to cost the price of running the appliances for one hour during the day. They should then compare the prices with night-time costs.

Which appliances would it be sensible and cheaper to use during the night on Economy 7?
- Encourage the groups to consider other uses of electricity. For example, you can watch about six hours of television for one unit of electricity. How many hours could you watch for £0.50 using the daytime tariff? Let the children choose and then list the programmes they would like to watch. Given £1.00 to spend, invite them to plan the programmes over a week.
- Encourage the children to devise their own questions. As well as providing links with science and technology, this area of work offers many opportunities for research and will encourage children to plan and develop their own mathematics.

4. House expenses

Age range
Ten to twelve.

Group size
Pairs or small groups.

What you need
Calculators, pencils, paper, wallpaper price lists, room measuring charts.

What to do
Collect leaflets on wallpaper prices and room measuring charts from DIY shops. Most charts will show total lengths of walls in metres against the height of rooms. For example:

Number of rolls required

		Height of room in metres			
		1.8	2.1	2.4	2.7
	8	4	5	5	6
Total length	9	4	5	6	6
of walls	10	5	6	6	7
in metres	11	5	6	7	8
	12	6	7	8	8

Give the groups the dimensions of the room you want them to plan for, and a variety of wallpaper prices. For instance, roll (a) costs £3.80, roll (b) £4.70 and roll (c) £6.20. Ask them to produce estimates for decorating the room. Then ask them other questions. For example, how much would it cost to wallpaper the room yourself if you used wallpaper (b)? What would the cost be if you employed a decorator who charges £9.50 an hour, plus the cost of materials at the trade price of £4.00 a roll, plus VAT? The decorator estimates that it will take six hours to complete the work. How much would you save if you did it yourself?

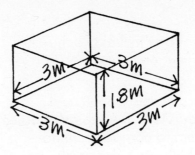

Total lengths of walls — 12m
Height of room — 1·8m
Rolls required — 6

Follow-up
• To carpet the floor of a room measuring 3 metres square, one carpet shop charges £12.50 a square metre plus a fitting charge of £15.00. Another carpet shop charges £15.00 a square metre plus free fitting. Ask the children which they would choose, and why.

• Ask the children to suppose that they want to refurnish a room. They decide to buy a three-piece suite and some new curtains. The curtains cost £120.00 and the suite costs £765.00. If they pay cash they can save 10%. How much will they pay?

Devise similar questions based on the total cost of decoration and furnishing. Ask the groups to design a room layout and choose the wallpaper and furnishings using catalogues and their own research to estimate the costs. They could then produce a scale model with a price list attached, which would link the investigation with technology.

5. Holidays

Age range
Ten to twelve.

Group size
Pairs or small groups.

What you need
Calculators, pencils, paper, holiday travel brochures.

What to do
Collect some holiday travel brochures from travel agencies. Discuss with the group how the tables of dates and prices are set out. Ask them to compare similar holidays to the same venue which are offered by different travel companies. Many interesting lines of investigation could arise from this topic. An example chart is given here which could act as a starting point for further work. The basic holiday prices per person are given in pounds.

Dates	Parama		Tasos	
	Self-catering		B & B	
	7 nights	14 nights	7 nights	14 nights
15–23 April	£153	£186	£153	£186
24–30 April	£168	£201	£168	£201
1–22 May	£175	£210	£180	£220
23–29 May	£190	£225	£200	£245

You could ask the children questions such as the following:
- How much would you save if you booked a holiday for two for seven days at Parama, departing on 15 April, as opposed to departing on 23 May?
- If you book your holiday before February you get a 15% reduction. How much would you save on a holiday at Tasos departing on 1 May for 14 days?

6. Route planner

Age range
Nine to eleven.

Group size
Six to eight children.

What you need
Calculators, pencils, paper, AA or RAC books, maps, car manuals.

What to do
Distances between towns can be found by using a mileage chart. Collect handbooks containing such charts from the various motoring organisations. Discuss with the groups how these charts are compiled and how to read them to find the distance between two places.

Challenge the groups to work out various routes around the country using a chart and a map of the British Isles. For example, suggest that they plan a round trip which involves visiting eight of the first division football grounds in England, starting in Birmingham. How many miles will be covered? Is it possible to plan more than one route? Which route would give the shortest distance to travel?

You can develop this type of activity using other contexts such as visiting shopping centres in different parts of the country or planning a pop group's tour of major city venues.

Follow-up
Once the groups have devised a travel plan and indicated the distances between each football ground, introduce a second element. Invite them to work out the cost of the journey. This could be calculated from information given in car manuals. Miles per gallon are usually shown alongside the engine capacity of the cars. The children could calculate different estimates for different types and models of car. Ask them to consider which car would be the cheapest to use.

This type of problem-solving exercise lends itself to many real-life situations. The children could consider planning deliveries between local towns, sight-seeing tours around their own county and many other situations.

Reproducible material

What does what? see page 9

Floating point

LCD

Function indicator

Memory add

Memory minus

Memory recall

Divide

Multiply

Minus

Add

Equals

Decimal point

Zero

Clear entire memory

Cancel last entry

Percentage

Reciprocal

Square root

Change sign

Auto power down

Memory in use indicator

Constant in use indicator

Negative number

Power on

AUTO SHUT OFF

Talking about calculator keys, see page 10

Equals	Nought
Clear entry	Shared by
Minus	Difference
Decimal point	Take away
Makes	Plus
Subtract	Multiply
Cancel everything	Lots of
Times	Divided by
Add	Product
Display	Zero
Sum	Total

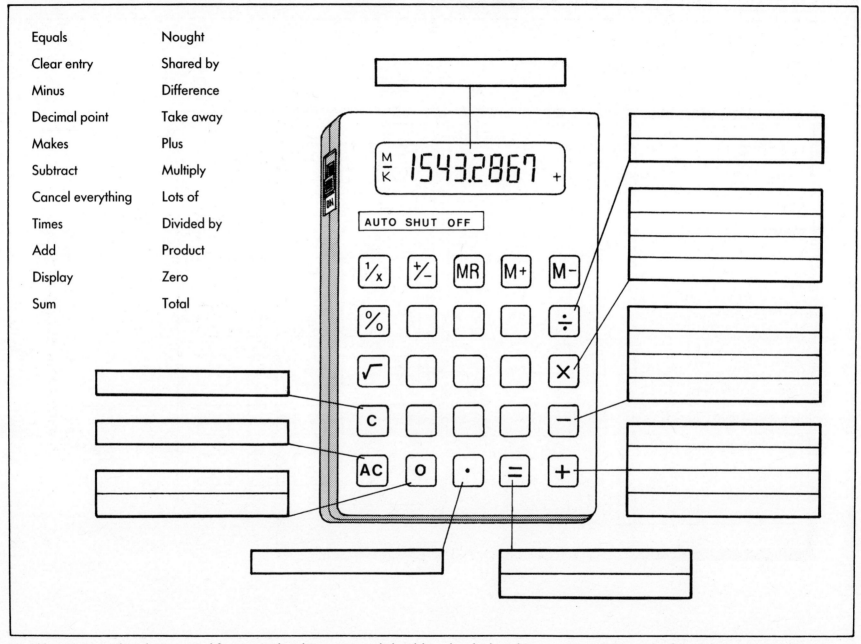

Calculator puppet, see page 23

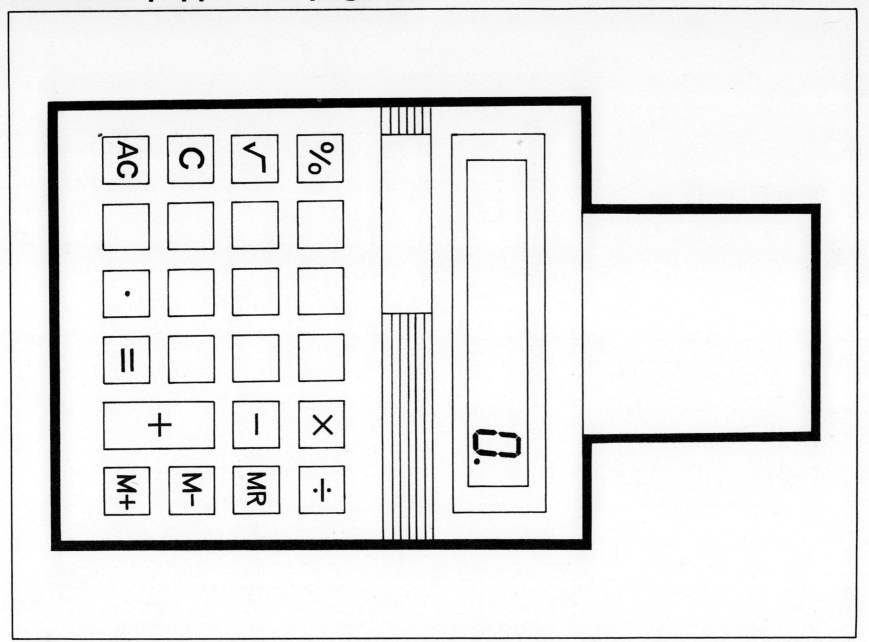

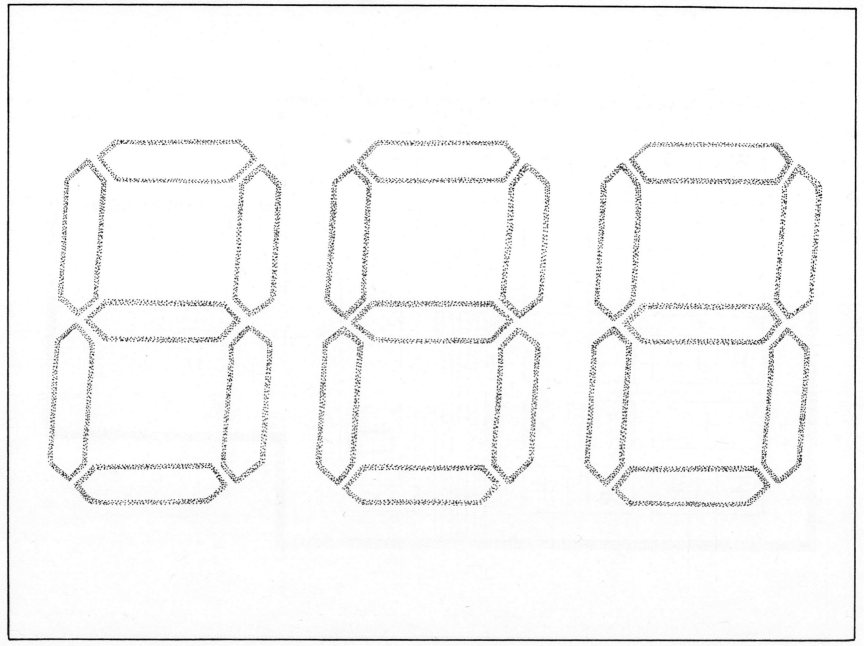

Using digital paper, see page 26

Numbers are fun! see page 28

Finish the sentence, see page 31

Answer numbers

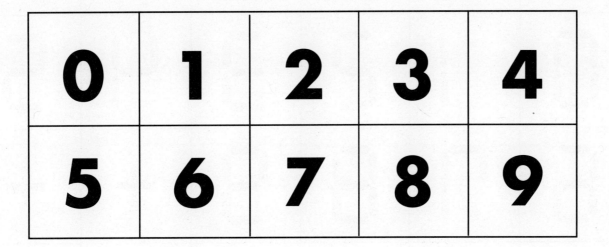

Finish the sentence, see page 31

Digital numbers

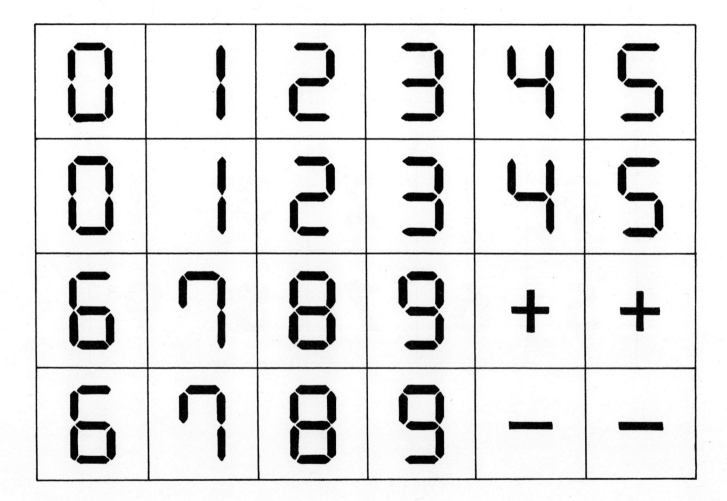

Finish the sentence, see page 31

Baseboard

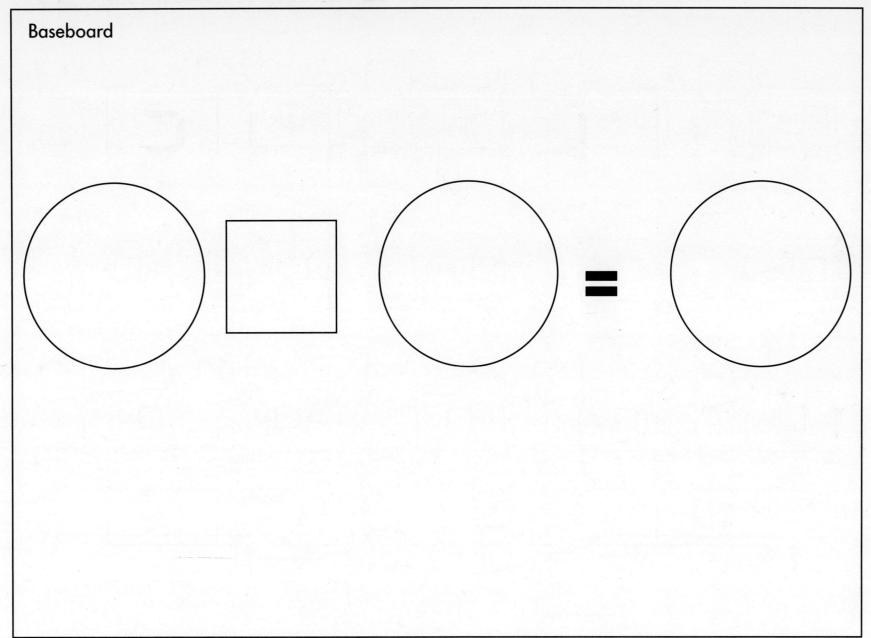

Win a bone, see page 31

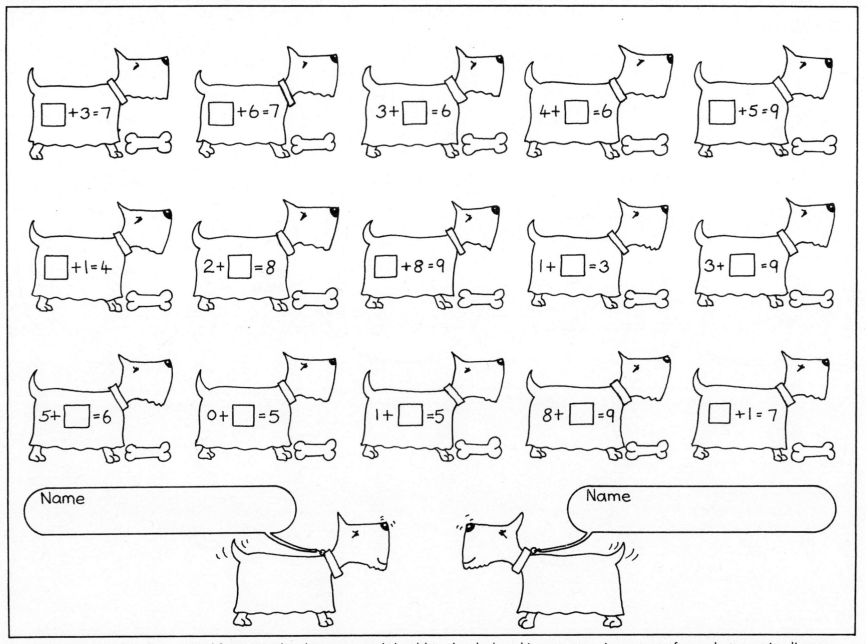

$\square + 3 = 7$

$\square + 6 = 7$

$3 + \square = 6$

$4 + \square = 6$

$\square + 5 = 9$

$\square + 1 = 4$

$2 + \square = 8$

$\square + 8 = 9$

$1 + \square = 3$

$3 + \square = 9$

$5 + \square = 6$

$0 + \square = 5$

$1 + \square = 5$

$8 + \square = 9$

$\square + 1 = 7$

Name

Name

Snakes, see page 32

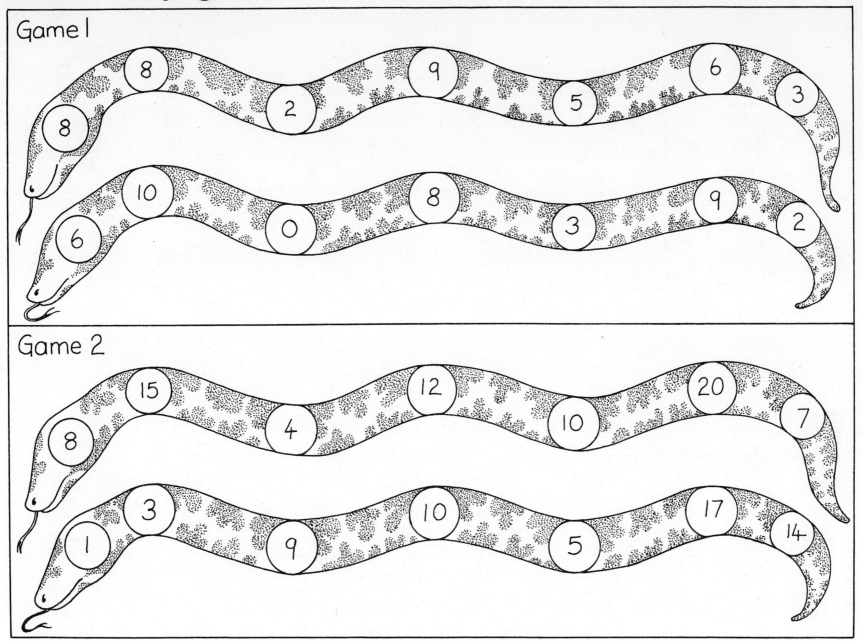

Game 1

Game 2

Frog jumps, see page 34

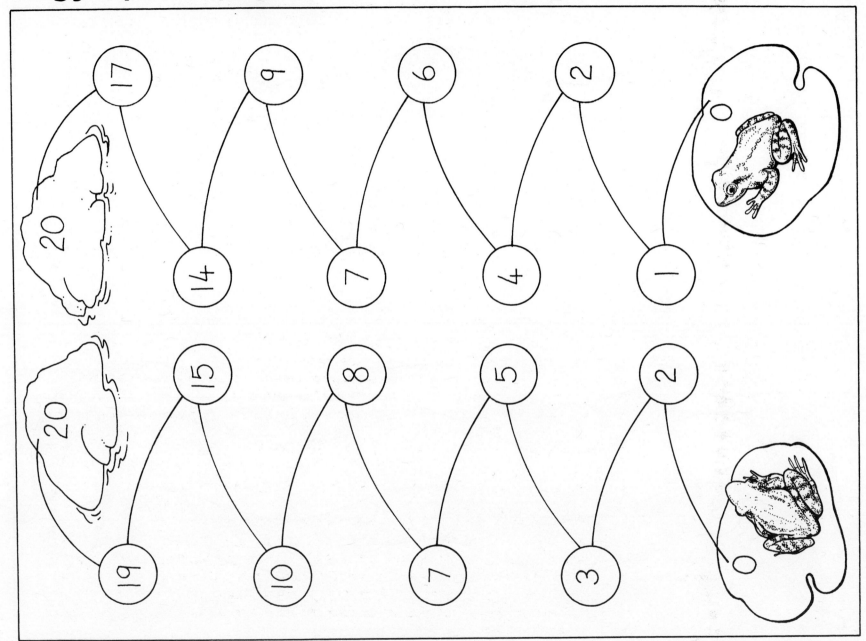

Match it, see page 34

Number Sentences

2+2 16+4 3+2 4+2 4+5 1+0 2+9 2+0 3+4 5+5 8+9 4+4

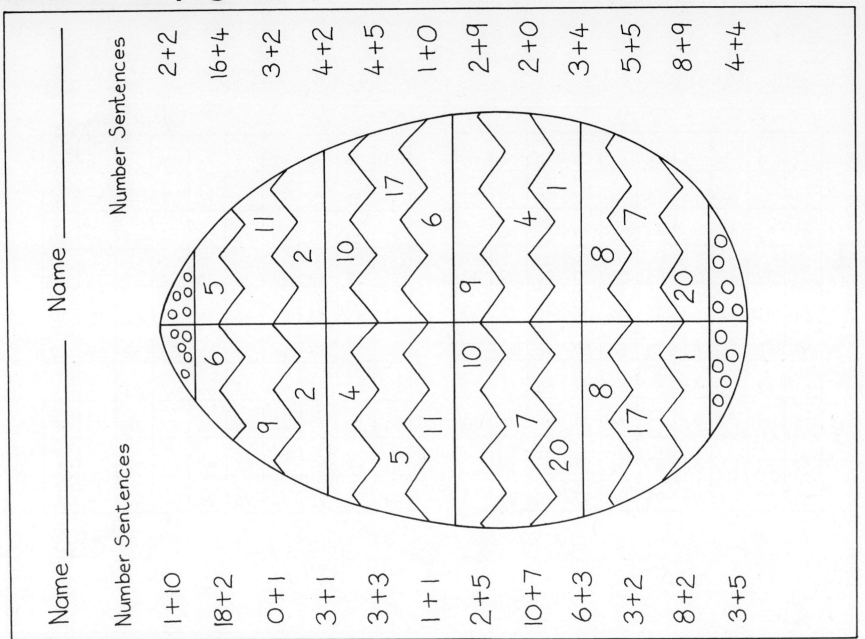

Name _____

Number Sentences

1+10 18+2 0+1 3+1 3+3 1+1 2+5 10+7 6+3 3+2 8+2 3+5

Number pattern squares, see page 38

1	2	3	4	5	6	7	8	9	10
11	12	13	14	15	16	17	18	19	20
21	22	23	24	25	26	27	28	29	30
31	32	33	34	35	36	37	38	39	40
41	42	43	44	45	46	47	48	49	50
51	52	53	54	55	56	57	58	59	60
61	62	63	64	65	66	67	68	69	70
71	72	73	74	75	76	77	78	79	80
81	82	83	84	85	86	87	88	89	90
91	92	93	94	95	96	97	98	99	100

1	2	3	4	5	6	7	8	9	10
11	12	13	14	15	16	17	18	19	20
21	22	23	24	25	26	27	28	29	30
31	32	33	34	35	36	37	38	39	40
41	42	43	44	45	46	47	48	49	50
51	52	53	54	55	56	57	58	59	60
61	62	63	64	65	66	67	68	69	70
71	72	73	74	75	76	77	78	79	80
81	82	83	84	85	86	87	88	89	90
91	92	93	94	95	96	97	98	99	100

Number lines, see page 39

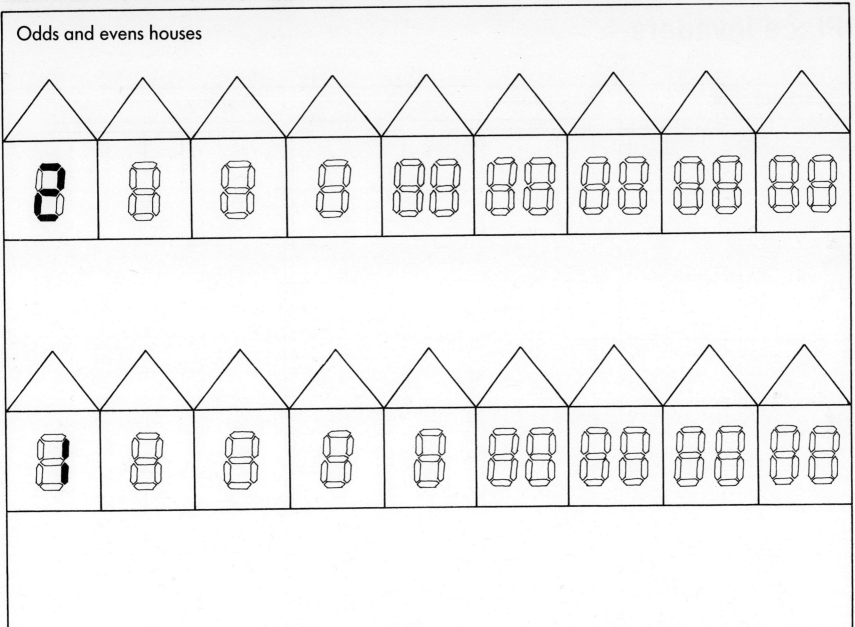

Odds and evens houses

Place invaders, see page 43

Place invaders

Start number	Key presses	Display

Follow the track, see page 49

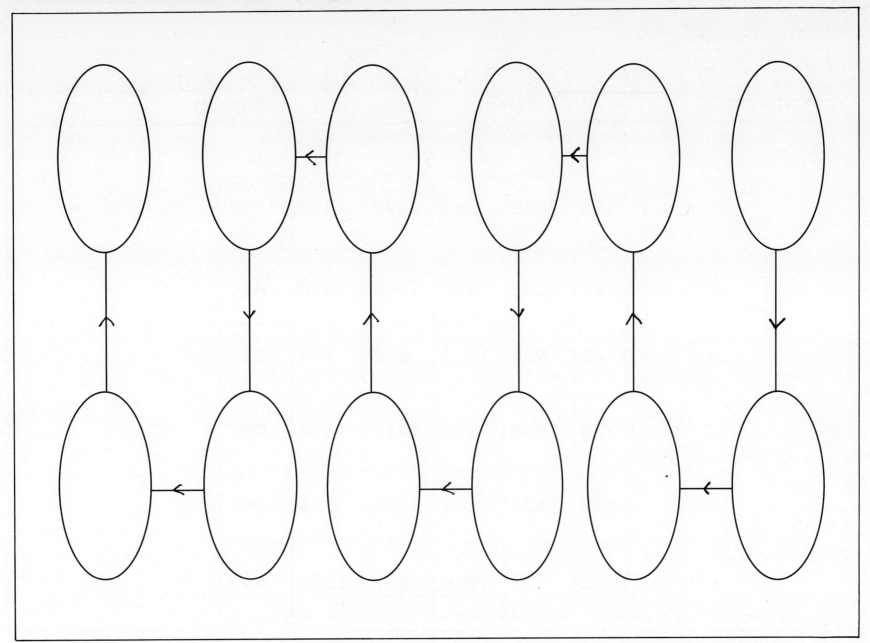

Lines of four, see page 63

17 21 25 28 31 37 41 42 44 x =

Use any of the numbers shown in the box above to try to make the numbers in the square. If you make the number you can cover it with one of your counters. The winner is the first person to make a row of four counters in any direction.

136	4882	861	1271	357	1722
777	1025	425	1804	1218	629
1189	924	1517	697	714	1554
775	1073	525	1211	527	925
748	1628	609	1147	725	899
1302	651	1276	1848	1050	493

Lines of four, see page 63

Use any of the numbers shown in the box above to try to make the numbers in the square. If you make the number you can cover it with one of your counters. The winner is the first person to make a row of four counters in any direction.

Rounding and multiplying

Question	Round both numbers up	Round both numbers down	Round first up and second down	Round first down and second up	Calculator check
8.31 x 6.94	9 x 7 = 63	8 x 6 = 48	9 x 6 = 54	8 x 7 = 56	57.6714
8.29 x 3.36					
5.13 x 7.58					
2.31 x 3.84					
4.56 x 2.92					
9.67 x 8.41					
3.29 x 4.26					

Estimate and multiply

Question	Estimated answer	Possible answers		Calculator check
3.82 x 5.4	4 x 2 = 8	4.0324 8.6714	0.4024 86.714	8.6714
11.7 x 5.4		63.18 73.58	52.48 84.68	
8.84 x 3.41		30.1444 26.4644	38.0214 42.6264	
12.26 x 7.94		86.3624 72.6314	108.7214 97.3444	

Number chains 1

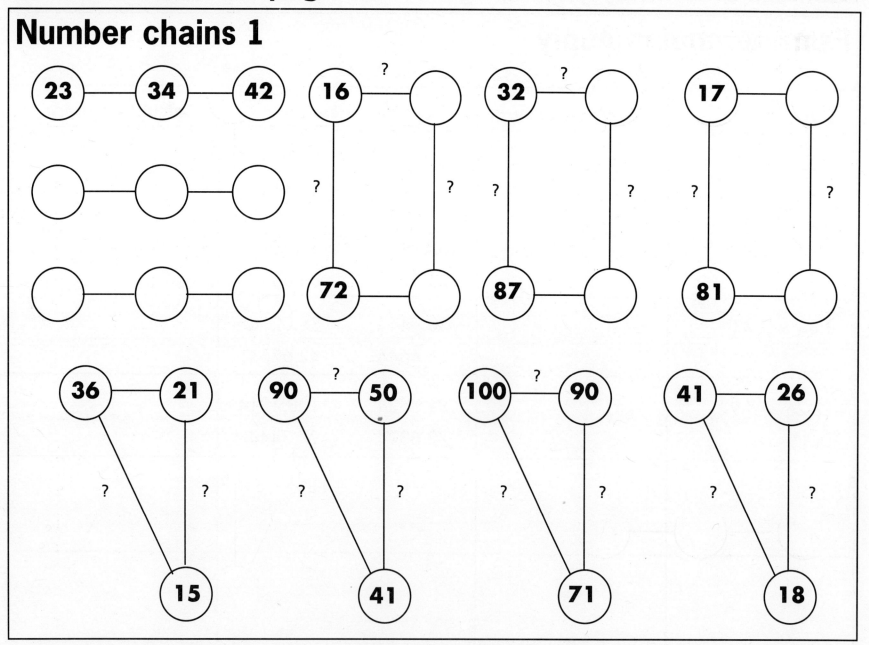

Number chains, see page 74

Number chains 2

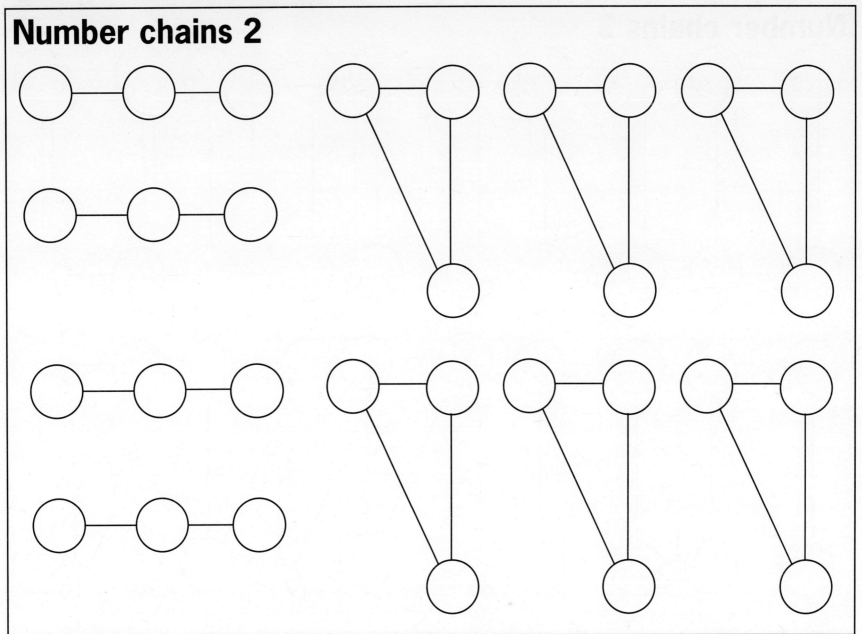

Number chains 3

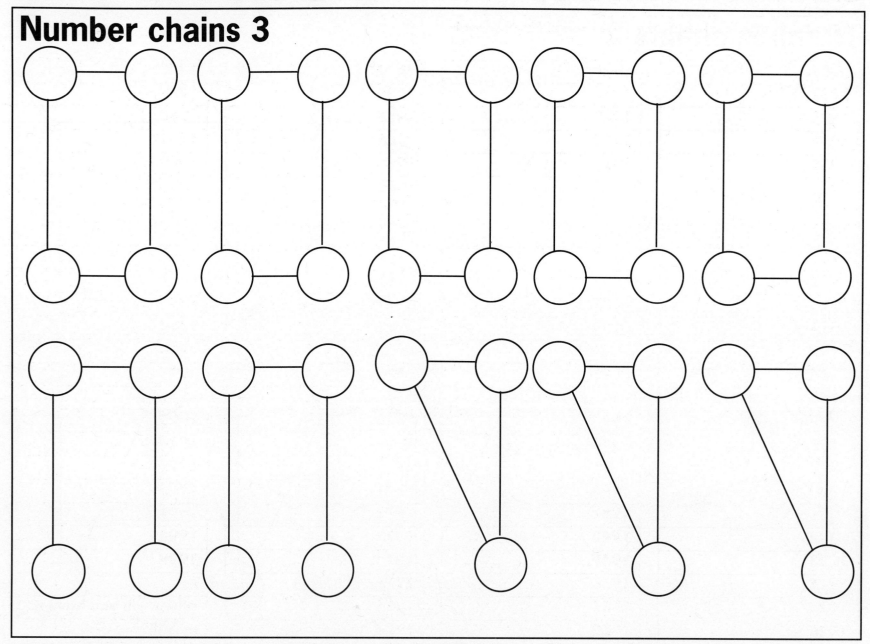

Grandmother's gift, see page 88

Round off to the nearest penny when completing the table.

1901	1927	1953	1978
1902	1928	1954	1979
1903	1929	1955	1980
1904	1930	1956	1981
1905	1931	1957	1982
1906	1932	1958	1983
1907	1933	1959	1984
1908	1934	1960	1985
1909	1935	1961	1986
1910	1936	1962	1987
1911	1937	1963	1988
1912	1938	1964	1989
1913	1939	1965	1990
1914	1940	1966	1991
1915	1941	1967	1992
1916	1942	1968	1993
1917	1943	1969	1994
1918	1944	1970	1995
1920	1946	1971	1996
1921	1947	1972	1997
1922	1948	1973	1998
1923	1949	1974	1999
1924	1950	1975	
1925	1951	1976	**When will you have a**
1926	1952	1977	**million pounds?**

Negative numbers, see page 89

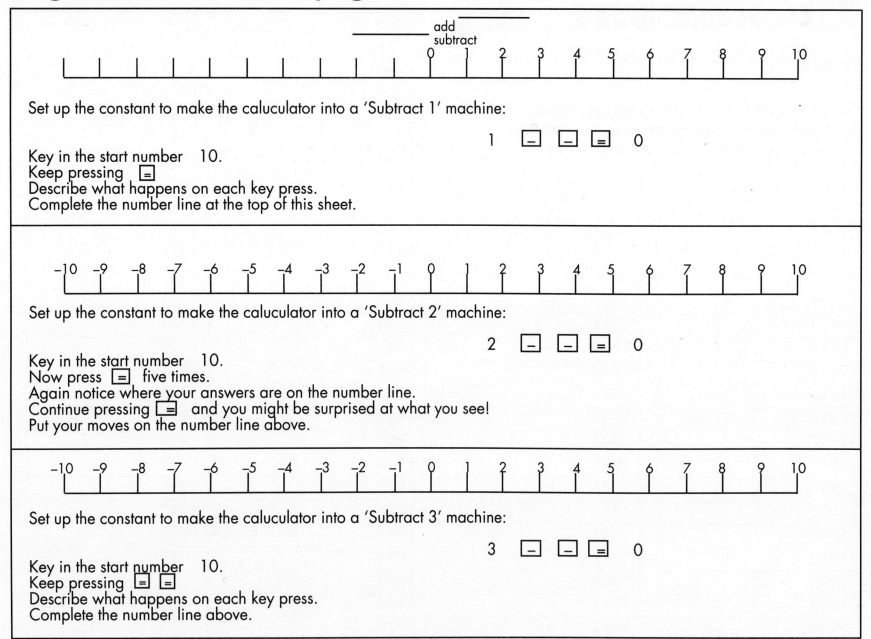

add
subtract

0 1 2 3 4 5 6 7 8 9 10

Set up the constant to make the caluculator into a 'Subtract 1' machine:

1 ⊟ ⊟ ⊟ 0

Key in the start number   10.
Keep pressing   ⊟
Describe what happens on each key press.
Complete the number line at the top of this sheet.

-10 -9 -8 -7 -6 -5 -4 -3 -2 -1 0 1 2 3 4 5 6 7 8 9 10

Set up the constant to make the caluculator into a 'Subtract 2' machine:

2 ⊟ ⊟ ⊟ 0

Key in the start number   10.
Now press   ⊟   five times.
Again notice where your answers are on the number line.
Continue pressing   ⊟   and you might be surprised at what you see!
Put your moves on the number line above.

-10 -9 -8 -7 -6 -5 -4 -3 -2 -1 0 1 2 3 4 5 6 7 8 9 10

Set up the constant to make the caluculator into a 'Subtract 3' machine:

3 ⊟ ⊟ ⊟ 0

Key in the start number   10.
Keep pressing   ⊟ ⊟
Describe what happens on each key press.
Complete the number line above.

Attainment target chart

Use this chart to help match up the activities outlined in this book with the relevant attainment targets for mathematics. The activities are identified by numbers; thus **2**/4 is Chapter 2, activity 4.

For the purposes of the chart we have used the attainment targets put forward in the *National Curriculum Council Consultation Report for Mathematics* (NCC 1991). The activities in this book will be of particular use in supporting work in AT 2 (Number) and AT 3 (Algebra), and the chart therefore sets out the links with these attainment targets. You will also find that many of the activities are relevant to the other targets, notably AT 1 (Using and applying mathematics).

This book will also support the Scottish *National Guidelines: Mathematics 5–14*, in particular the attainment outcomes of 'Problem solving and enquiry', 'Information handling' and 'Number, money and measurement'.

AT / Level	2	3
1	**2**/1, **2**/2, **2**/4, **2**/6, **2**/9, **2**/10, **2**/11, **3**/1, **3**/3, **4**/1	**2**/5
2	**3**/10, **4**/1, **4**/2, **4**/3, **4**/4, **4**/5	**3**/2, **3**/7, **3**/13, **4**/8, **4**/9
3	**3**/4, **3**/5, **3**/6, **3**/8, **3**/9, **3**/12, **4**/1, **4**/2, **4**/3, **4**/4, **4**/5, **4**/6, **4**/10, **5**/1, **5**/2, **5**/3, **5**/4, **6**/1, **7**/5, **8**/12	**3**/11, **4**/8, **4**/9, **7**/2, **7**/4
4	**4**/2, **4**/3, **4**/4, **4**/7, **5**/2, **5**/5, **5**/6	**5**/9, **7**/1, **7**/2
5	**4**/6, **5**/5, **5**/9, **6**/1, **6**/7, **6**/8, **6**/9, **6**/10, **6**/11, **6**/12, **7**/3, **8**/13, **8**/14, **8**/15	**7**/4, **7**/6
6	**4**/6, **5**/3, **5**/4, **5**/6, **5**/7, **5**/8, **5**/10, **6**/2, **6**/3, **6**/4, **6**/5, **6**/6, **6**/7, **6**/8, **8**/7, **8**/8, **8**/9, **8**/10, **8**/11	